KISS MY PATH

BOOK 1

The Emerald Path

By

Christine Janette

aka. C.J. Badger

Book Info

Kiss My Path: The Emerald Path, Book 1

Copyright ©2017

The names of people in this book have been changed except when representing historical fact, or were given express permission to include their stories are presented.

Cover design by Christine Janette Copyright ©2017

Cover courtesy of iStock Photo and Adobe Stock, artist Nikki Zlewski

Self-Published in the United States of America by Christine Janette

aka. C.J. Badger

ISBN: 978-0-9990832-0-8 (PAPERBACK)

ISBN: 978-0-9990832-1-5 (HARDBACK)

# Chapters

# Prelude

*Keeping Infinite Spirit Simple*

*A story of redefining our discovery, manifestation, and expansion, one kiss from Infinite Spirit at a time.*

*A kiss is a gentle spark from spirit, a call to action, a loving feeling and blessing.*

*A sign from Spirit when speech becomes unessential. When we receive a holy kiss from Spirit and the world stops, we listen in anticipation for Spirit to speak.*

*A kiss of nothing but love. A Spirit Kiss is an affirmation, sealed in the soul imparted from pure spirit.*

*Enlightenment is simply awakening to our own Spirit. It is our ability to know what is true within our self.*

*It is knowledge, insight, intuition, and wisdom. It becomes your own voice and purpose, our own weirdness.*

*It is a blessed state, marked with an absence of misgivings and fear.*

*It was not my path you kissed,*

*But my Soul*

# Dedication

I offer this book to the universe and beyond.

With all my love and devotion.

May it be used in the Creator's service in accordance with divine will to aid in the universal mission here on the green planet.

May it bring about only the highest benevolent good for all beings of free will.

Infinite Love and Much Gratitude

For You

I offer this book to you, with much love and devotion.

May it be used in service for you in harmony with the divine will to aid the universal mission.

For the innocent, hero, caregiver, seeker, rebel, lover, artist, joker, sage, healer, magician, and role models.

For the incarnate reader in bodily form.

For those who seek solace and comfort or happiness and joy.

For those needing hope and faith.

For those who have put out the vibration in the collective unconscious.

May it bring about the highest benevolent good for all free will beings.

## Introduction

Are you a good witch, or are you a bad witch? Well, I am not a witch at all. Although I have been called by many names, Bruja, sorceress, beautiful wife, friend, mother, mom, mommy, granddaughter, and Yaya. One of my favorites is just my nickname Chrissi. Although my first words into the introduction of this book may seem fitting to a story of the great and powerful OZ, this story, my story, is also story of discovery and finding our way home through healing, lessons, love, destiny, and the path that lead me to tell my story. Well, I guess that does sound a little like Dorothy's story, although mine may be a bit more treacherous and heart wrenching: on these pages there will be the retelling of tears. My recollections may be sporadic at times, however my information emerged to discover my way, my soul, and my purpose. You may receive senses of "been there, done that," or "this ain't my first rodeo."

This story is about my past and possibly your own. As you read my story among my shadows, things may leap out from the pages and seem to align with your own path, with your own life disasters, blessings, and misadventures. Most of us have had setbacks or strokes of bad luck, but all of this is inexorable for re-balancing and finding our who we really are. Finding our way home, down the golden road.

After reading my tale, you may think that I was dealt a shitty hand. That is far from the truth. I practice viewing everything as a blessing, viewing the situation for what it is trying to communicate to me, or an unbroken reminder of the blessings I have been given. Yeah, I'm not always a fucking ray of sunshine. I have my days, but Spirit is always there to remind me and get me back on my path.

In the present time, in the now, I have become more open to listening more often. Setting aside the time to listen is the key. Some may call it meditation, some deep thought, others self-examination. Do whatever works best for you in finding that place where you can open up and listen.

It goes without saying that my past lives have shaped and molded my existence now, developing the what "I AM" today. I have had to start over many times, in this life and in past lives. Each time something more magnificent has come about or has been discovered. My gifts keep giving, and I AM open to receiving them by the grace of God. I AM a genuinely blessed weirdo with much love (x's 3) and infinite gratitude for all my time spent on this planet. In my past lives, I believe I have been a witch, back in the era of the witch burnings. I discovered that I did not survive a drowning by ship. I have been a type of spiritual leader, (or maybe that is a voodoo priestess, I do love root work). I was also a mother that abandoned her child.

What I intend to do with this book and the books that follow is to touch you in some healing way, to aid in the search for your own soul, your own destiny. My past is full of kept secrets that have been unlocked: secrets and discoveries that unfolded before me by using my gifts and natural talents. There were gifts of self-discovery. I put that self-discovery into action and read between the lines, questioning and seeking everything in my life. Listening, seeing and recognizing the signals.

I have been listening to my inner voice that has been speaking to me my whole life through books, movies, music, tarot, numerology, astrology, and crystal vibrations. I seek any type of energy I can get my hands on and see it for what it genuinely is trying to tell me. "Pay attention to me, Lady," or as my grandson says, "listen to me Yaya..." Yes, I have been knocked around in the head a few times, both physically and spiritually.

The "key" is in the experience to arrive at the destination. That is, we must listen for the whispers from our guides, our angels, or departed loved ones. We can sometimes hear it in the voices of the living when we truly listen.

I will take you through my life from the beginning as a young child, and into my adulthood. Early on in life, I had to become the woman I thought I was, thinking I was all knowing. Who I really was is very different from the woman I AM today, knowing further and allowing my wisdom to grow. Know this now, forgiveness is a "key," the key to a light and open heart, and bringing love into your life no matter the experience. To forget on the other hand, is a different story. I don't believe we ignore what does not need to be forgotten, and we hold onto certain things waiting for that experience to come up at another point in life to allow it to be heale. These things can be forgotten and put back into the shallows of our minds and we will enable ourselves to move on to the next cycle life throws our way: the NOW, the I AM.

To spice things up, I have added a little dialogue about my experience with past life regression. This spice is the added ingredient that has made me the character I am today. I feel so blessed to know these things about myself, and they have helped me get through some tough times, as well as some fun experiences and adventures.

This book is me screaming. Screaming at my heart center into the evolution of me, from my heart chakra. The green heart chakra, the color of love, and the path I have been on. My next book will be an exploration of the blue chakra. To "communicate" with you other gifts that may be similar to your own ascensions, that is, I am referring to the awakening of Kundalini, our life source, our soul paths What the world needs now is some awakening, some advances in consciousness. I am doing my part in service to perhaps touch someone else seeking the same. I have awakened from my slumber, many times over I might add. Communications from the one source are opening up to me at lightning speeds, nudging me to listen to my inner voice, and my guided wisdom.

The Universe has been asking me to share my story and how I use my gifts and tools. We all get these intuitive nudges, impulses, and desires: God speaks to us in many different ways beyond rational process. You may call this force something other than God, such as spirit, intuition, angels, or ancient aliens. I will stick with the term God, for the most part, throughout the books. I have learned to just keep it simple and stick with what I know, having sat alone at the edge of my awareness and fear. I have had the debilitating feeling of the inability to share, of having other feelings overcome me, like excitement, heart vibration, and hot flashes (yes and not because I am an old crone). I have had the blissful feeling of knowing who I AM. The sense that it is now time to share this with those of you that are asking questions, asking for a story, asking for a manual: A "how to" to help one unravel your own mysteries, your own soul purposes and your own destinies. This is a simple book to help you communicate and begin to see for yourself how to use symbols, art, and poetry, words in a book, animals, and the voices in your head, the gut feelings, and the heartstrings. I will leave out the scary voices, I will leave those voices and words to the writers of horror stories. I haven't any space for those voices any longer. I have no more room for fear. I choose to leave fear in the past. As my grandson says, "enough Yaya" (there is so much wisdom in that little boy). Out of the mouths of babes, I now recognize my inner child.

We don't have to look any further than our own backyards, wherever your yard is at this time, at this moment. You have the tools now, with you at any moment. Ask, and you shall receive, ask for anything you want and receive it. Be open to receiving. NOW, not yesterday, not tomorrow, right this minute, second, hour... Follow the path that has been under your feet all this time. Follow the path that will lead you to your purpose, to get back home if you are lost. Follow the road to love. Put on the ruby slippers, the heart clock, the red badge of courage, the red ribbon of decree. Follow your essential inner knowing! Trust in yourself as God has trusted in you. Trust in your God-self.

Walk with me on my journey, won't you? With songs and gospels of rainbows, with nature and the animals, with art, and the reading and writings on the wall. Our DNA is begging us . . . Our angels are calling, Spirit is speaking, blowing gentle kisses that spark from the Soul. The earth needs the blessed weird ones to come forth. The rebels, the lovers, the creators, the sages, and the jesters. Our human experience needs a good house cleaning to get the bats out of the belfry. We need to rise up and follow our breadcrumbs to ascension, find our tribes, work together to create a new peace with free will for all.

This book is not a self-help read, but a book of self-realization. It is a guide to both a galaxy far, far away and the one right in front of you. I will use the phrases I AM, I Intend, me, we, you, and us. You will hear music, read quotes, and urban slang that may speak to you in many different ways. Take it with a grain of salt, so to speak. Now take a few deep breaths and let's begin. Raise the chalice and "may the Saints bless your pints!" Here's to reading between the lines, and riding the edge. It is what is needed

right now!

I would like to share with you an excerpt of one of my favorite books and authors:

Blessed Are the Weird, A Manifesto for Creatives

by Jacob Nordby

You have left a trail of breadcrumb clues that will lead you to the place where your purpose and passion have already met and are simply waiting for you to find them.

# Chapter 1

# The Emerald Path

*That moment when the voice is calling. To choose
the path that will lead me to the hidden path within
myself, heading into the unknown by faith alone.*

I have a tonality that has awakened in me. I call it the
Kundalini, the life force that resides in me, the snake, a process, an
alteration from my past, and a small list of past lives. I call it a
creative being wishing to be discovered. My story is a piece of art
slithering up my spine like a snake on fire. Passing through each
Chakra, each color, and every vibration. A Warrior Queen of great
inner magic waiting to be re-birthed from the depth of my soul.

For years I held onto trying to fix everyone around me, to
nurture everyone else, knowing deep down that I can only do so
when myself is nurtured when I begin to heal myself. A person can
only lead another to water. You cannot make them drink...that
would be drowning. Some things just can't be fixed. I know this

from experience; the fear can be just too deep. We can only heal

what is asked of us. If you look into the dark waters, your

reflection can reveal what needs to be healed if you look deep

enough. All the magic and spells in the world can't heal someone

until they are undeniably willing. We can get burned at the stake if

we are not careful. We can become a high shamanic priestess,

working with our tribes, working within the circle of what we

know and what we can fix our specialties and our vocations.

My references above are from deep within myself, my past

lives. I have known my past lives for many years. Deju Vu doo all

the time. Drowning was a recollection of a previous life. As a child

someone tried drowning me, a few people actually, I'm sure they

thought it was funny holding someone's head under the water. I

have never been able to watch The Titanic or read about it. It gives

me the willies.

Fear and hate are a part of a past matrimony. Sometimes

revenge for abandonment just goes too deep, back into past lives.

This is but only one of the reasons I left my ex-husband. A psychic

once told me if I did not we would have killed one another.

Apparently, he was my child in a past life, and I abandoned him, he was still angry with me for something beyond my control. A burning at the stake, yep... a witch, or what I like to call an herbalist or rootworker. I have always had way too much interest in this. My life has always pushed me to study and practice holistic healing in many modalities, in many different circles. Through the use of divinity, prayer, affirmations and I AM presence.

With a pen, paper, and keyboard, I am putting my story out there. Do with it what you will decide what you know and what you connect with. I was asked to write this book, so I AM. I AM unpacking my baggage, my innermost secrets, sharing some gifts and tools. Please, enjoy the show.

*~Trapped in my Soul~*

*My mind can't imagine anything*

*Trapped in my Soul*

*My mind keeps on telling me*

*You need to meet the divine*

*Every time I try to unwrap*

*My mind keeps on telling*

*My Dear, you've been trapped*

*Feelings of internal conflict*

*Love and Fear*

*My mind keeps on telling me*

*You must rise and hear*

*Now my soul is telling me*

*HEY! You want that*

*I say, well of course I do*

*My Soul keeps on telling me*

*You are such a brat!*

All my feelings and musings have wanted to burst out into something creative. They have been trapped in my soul, my soul has desired me to set the creative weirdo free. I have been that person that holds everything inside because everyone else's needs have been put before mine. I did this always thinking I was doing the right thing and not living my dreams and wishes. I wasn't sure what that really was until now. Now is the time...The time to unlock the door to my soul and set it free. Now is the time to begin creating the rest of my life. My inner child goes into things kicking and screaming. Now is the time for this spiritual brat to find her creative side, unleash her magic, and share the tools. I need to clear the closets, leaving just the necessities so that I may move on to create the rest of my time.

For most of my life, I have created a sacred space of my own: An area that would just belong to me whether that was a two-by-two jail bed, a corner of the couch, or a beautiful loft in the upstairs of my home. I made it mine; I learned to use this space to begin creating, to learn and gain wisdom, and to divine. My tools for divining have been many. I used to draw upon my many varieties of tarot cards, animal medicine cards, crystal vibration books, numerology, and astrology.

In the two-by-two (just a figure of speech) jail bed I used prayer and affirmations. I tried using my stepfather to get me out. He would not have it, would not lift a finger to help me. Denied me yet again, abandoned me in my time of need, the only time I have ever needed him. The vessel that brought me into this world thought it a good idea to deny me as well. I needed to learn a lesson, the vessel proclaimed, or I should say her psychic told her. "You were drinking too much," was her opinion, I was placed there not by alcohol directly (more on this in chapters ahead). I needed these tools to keep me safe, to keep me sane. I used my tools to pull me out of many funks, many despairs, and any discouragement. They were always there to validate who I am and kept me on track. I cannot say they failed me, I failed them, I failed me. But then again, did I fail? For without failures you can't really become close to God and know love. Screaming his name in the seduction of sex doesn't get you closer. Believe me, I have tested this theory; it only gets you closer to climax. Failure and fear are what moved me closer. God said we have Love and Fear. You cannot know one without the other.

I have carried and held onto the things that are important to me and have divine importance. I have managed to hold on to these things going through homelessness, and the many moves throughout my life. Holding them close and dear to me the tools that give me solace. I had tiny boxes, satchels, and suitcases in which I put my treasures in, my gifts. I still have many of them to this day, only letting go of them when they no longer are of service to me or had been lost or stolen. Stolen by those who determined they must have needed it more than I, and that is okay, you are forgiven. I understand, for I too have stolen to meet my needs. Things can be replaced, with new things. I have managed a pretty sizable collection of books that speak to me with all the highlighted rainbow colors and notes I have filled the pages with. Going back to them quite often because I know where to find things, I know how to fix things. I know this because I know how things work. My Tarot and Animal Medicine card collections have come to my rescue many times. To view at face value my present situation and guide me through it. For this, I am blessed.

Picture a child as happy, secure, and dancing on the earth without a care. In the backdrop, there is a stone house and a mighty oak. The child longs for the parent figures but feels she is on her own and alone in many ways. Pausing to look around to find her heart, her love. There is also something she senses, something of the unknown. "Where can I find this "thing"?" I do believe this thing has to do with unconditional love, and knowing who she is...who she really is. Not really ever fitting into any social picture of a typical child. But what...what is she? Where does she begin her search?

Let's begin by introducing the child. Imagine her with fair hair, green eyes, and she is just two years old. She is jumping in mud puddles in the front of the house. An old home in a cul-de-sac, one of her favorite places to be. A favorite part of the house is the closet, the one closest to the front door. The closet contains an old umbrella of the man that lived there before, so she was told. She thinks it is magical and it would help her to fly. She uses it to amuse the chipmunks, dancing around their cage in the backyard.

She could see they looked so pitiful in the cage and wanted to be free, they looked thirsty.

One day she found a 7-Up bottle and filled it with water, and tried to give them water to drink. That did not go over too well with her aunt, who snitched on her. Boy did she get into trouble? She said they were thirsty and needed water...She knew they needed water and wanted to be free. She received a good spanking for that. This place didn't seem so magical to her any longer. She wasn't heard; all she got was her ass set afire. Her place of escape from her actual home life, a hotel where she slept on a cot, in the corner of the kitchen. This was a place where her only play area was right in front, outside the door. There was a small piece of cement where she could play with her kitchen and pretend to be a mommy and have a home with her prince charming. Then one day her prince showed up. He was a boy that lived in the hotel as well. They would play for hours, outside on the cold cement. Cooking and talking about the kinds of things two-year-olds talk about. Saving the world, making a peaceful existence, who was going to change their diaper? It was as if he was sent to play with her and they would know each other the rest of their lives. This playful time did not last long either, and she never saw him again. What did you expect? They were just two years old, barely able to speak the language of adults.

We moved several more times after that. I began to think I was a gypsy traveling in a wagon from place to place. Running into a creepy old man in his car playing with his nuts and talking to my friend and me about eggplant. I had a dreary, uneventful conversation with the police that night. From what I recall it wasn't long after that we moved again. Leaving friends behind again.

I was in Kindergarten now, and we moved out to the country amongst the thoroughbred horses and dairy cows. We lived behind the large areas of green grasses where the horses grazed, down a long road to our little home on the ranch. I don't know when this happened. I don't recall the vessel being pregnant. But then again, I think I was an immaculate conception. I now have two younger sisters, I somehow missed the birth of them and don't remember them too much as babies except in photos. I do remember sitting on the steps with them, being told to keep an eye on them (I was about five or six), and I did.

I would shoo-away the flies from landing on their little faces. I knew they were mine to take care of and be there for. I looked after them, to have them to look up to me. I learned some things on my visit here, this home on the ranch. I learned not to get involved in other people's shenanigans and how to find my way home, kind of. I think this was when I began to feel out of place, weird, and alone.

We were having lunch in the cafeteria as any regular first-grade class does. You see, I just graduated from graham crackers and milk to cafeteria food lines. No more taking naps on towels on a cold cement school floor for me. I was excited; I was a big girl now. I somehow became involved in a straw-shooting ring. The other kids were shooting them back and forth via forced air into one end of the straw. I did not want to be involved in this, so I just offered it back to them. I did not want to get into to any trouble, but somehow I did, I was the scapegoat. I was at the wrong place and the wrong time. I went down for the crime. I was laid on top of a table, in front of the whole class, and got the yardstick to my ass.

Again my ass was set afire. I didn't ever want to go back to that school.

I was far from the princess that my aunts played dress up with. I was a pauper getting punished for something I had no control over or even participated in. I was lost. Really, I got lost. The vessel thought it was a good idea for me to learn how to take the bus, to remember which one to get onto to get home to the ranch. I ended up on my only friend's bus, at her house with her family. I decided to walk home from there, I knew the way... so I thought. Luckily the vessel and the principal found me on a country road, heading home, wherever I thought that may be. I was heading someplace, I was sure of myself. I guess I have always just been in tune with my path. I have a good sense of direction. I get off track sometimes, taking the side roads, but there is always a path that leads to home, the Emerald Path, the path way to Love.

# Chapter Two

# A Place Called Home

How ironic, we finally moved into a stable home. I entered into first grade here; however, the school year had begun. We lived on Home Street. Really, that was the name of the street. We lived there for the next five or so years of my life in the 70s. It was family friendly, had lots of kids, and was a very nationality diverse neighborhood. I had lived in every single bedroom of this house. We had beautiful green lawns, the most vibrant, colorful flower garden and rose beds out in the front yard. I loved our Queen Elizabeth roses. Honestly the old man's pride and joy. In the backyard, we had plenty of room to play, a beautiful lawn, vegetable garden, a swing set, a patio, small pool in the summer, and a greenhouse, which was off limits to us kids (wink-wink). Each room was painted a different color: blue, green, yellow, and the brown room. The brown room scared me. It seemed like it was always cold and dark. It eventually ended up being my middle sister's bedroom. Maybe that is why she was always crying. My sisters and I shared this room at first before it was painted brown.

Why would anyone put children in a brown room is beyond me. It wasn't even a nice brown, it was a mustardy brown. There were no curtains at the time. We had only been here a short while, and the vessel still had some sprucing up to do.

One night after us girls was tucked into bed for the evening; I lay there trying to fall asleep, a man came to the window. I am not sure why or who, or if he was even real. Could he have been an angel? He stood there and stared into the room for a while, brushed at his hair, and walked off. I lay there scared, my heart racing not knowing what to do but to lie there as if I was asleep as if I was invisible. I willed him away, with all my might, eyes shut tight. My eyes were closed tight, but just peeking through my eyelashes, actually I was squinting. "There is nothing to see here," I said in my head. Leave my girls and me alone. He did, he walked off into the light of the full moon. I wanted a new room or at least some drapes. Why had creeps always found their way to me, or was he just watching over me?

The room I felt most joyful in was the yellow room, with sheer daisy curtains. It was my little escape. It was in the very back of the house. It contained my stuffed animals and my writing desk.

I loved my writing desk. It had my treasures and secrets all hidden in drawers, awaiting my return from school or outside adventures. Back in those days, we didn't come back into the house until the streetlights went on.

I did a lot of journaling there on my little desk. I did a lot of imagining and dreaming. The curtains were white and sheer. I could see the moon dancing above on many nights. I would sleep beneath the moon and the stars. I would dream of the life I wanted, the dreams that most girls dream: to have children, lots of children. I seem to remember the magic number was five. I had to find my prince. I just knew he was out there, probably right in my own neighborhood.

For many years, I had a stuffed frog that I kissed goodnight. I also had a stuffed mouse that would one day turn into my illustrious horse and carry me away in my golden carriage. I dreamed of being free-spirited and blessed. The truth of it all was, although I would dream up these fab stories of the life I wanted, I never really did fit in anywhere with anyone for very long. Kids made fun of me in school. Called me names like Dumbo ears and

Pinocchio-nose. I never did fit into any one crowd or group. I had a few friends, don't get me wrong, they would come and go. I never really felt I even belonged to my own family. I felt more like a mother figure to my little sisters. We had a mom, the one I call "the vessel"; the one who gave us life. She would tuck us in at night and kiss our foreheads. My younger sisters are three and four years younger than I.

There just seemed like something was missing. I was always wondering where I belonged. I was always dreaming of a large green lawn, with big oak trees big enough for a swing. I imagined a comfortable home, most all girls dream of castles and being princesses. I felt more like Cinderella at times, keeping the chores up, feeding the girls. I grew up way too fast. Don't get me wrong, I love the vessel, but she has always been more of a friend or sister than a "mom" in my mind past the age of fourteen. I remember the vessel sleeping a lot, always napping. The old man always working, drinking, and what he called shade-treeing. Oh, he found time to teach us some things like "you don't know your ass from a hole in the ground," or "don't be a horse's ass." He was proud of the fact that he had three girls: a blond, a brunette, and a redhead. There were always gatherings at the house. We had family friends, the Portuguese friends, who would come over for some beers and smoke funny cigarettes. You know, the stuff in the "greenhouse." I never really felt a connection with the old man, I think he tried, I really do. I never felt he was my co-creator. I never felt unloved by the vessel. That is, she had love, just different ways of showing it, not by any fault of her own I guess. I will leave that there for now, for she has her own story to be told.

What I learned at this stage of life on Home Street was how to nurture, how to write out my dreams, and how to pray. I learned to nurture myself and my sisters. While the vessel napped and did her "manifesting," I learned to cook, clean, and pick up dog poop. I was a pretty good cook at a young age. I learned that if you don't take care of something, it ends up in the pound. I learned how to write, how to read the instructions on the tampon box all on my own. I learned how to make mean oatmeal, tasty spaghetti, and the best tacos. To this day I love to cook.

I did enjoy making oatmeal for my sisters; I was playing mommy. I learned that angry drunk men turn into monsters that like to knock people around. I learned that when this monster came after the vessel, she came running to me, in my room, as a safe haven. What was I supposed to do? I remember my two little sister's faces. One of them was always crying with her mouth wide open; the other was always running to me to stop the other from either scratching or biting. These two girls were always fighting. They were just mean to each other. One funny memory was when my littlest sister wanted to run away because she got in trouble for something. I think she was just five, maybe younger. I would not allow her to run away, so we made her a closet fort. We strung up a flashlight on the closet rod with a string and laid down blankets for her to sleep in. That lasted two hours. She had her time out.

What I really liked and miss in those younger years was writing in my diary. I enjoyed writing in my diary, it was my getaway, my time. I had several diaries. It was the place I wrote out my dreams and the conversations I had with myself. "Dear Diary...." I would be curious to read them now, to see how much of my conversations with God have come to fruition. Or how much derailing from my dreams I have done. These pieces of my early years are no longer in my possession, having lost them over the years. The diary was a place I could let things go. Where I could be thankful, where I could let out my anger for the day because I got into "trouble" for something I did not understand. Or why the old man was always so mean, or what was he so mad at?

I always wrote at the end of the day, before bed, hoping to have my prayers answered. In the morning it would all be a new start, a new beginning to a new day. My imagination, my room, my diary, and the books I read were my escape. I read The Hobbit, Tale of Two Cities, Beverly Cleary, and Old Mother Goose stories. These years were some of the best I had if you can believe that. I had a place to create, a place to plan out what I wanted when I grew up. This was the place I could be a child, a place called home.

I learned how to get it all out, say my grace, and forgive. I could solve the puzzles of life in my diary, in my room... My imagination has always served me as an escape and as a prisoner. This home is where I lost my virginity, (don't judge). This home is where I first laid eyes on my soul mate, where I learned secrets of myself. Where I became a young lady. I know this, I was told this time and time again: "Now listen here, young lady." After this, I didn't resume my journaling until my thirties. I am not quite sure why I stopped. Maybe some of my life needed to come to fruition and my wishes fulfilled. You know the saying, "be careful what you wish for." Words have power. I know this now.

The place I truly felt a "place called home" and at home, was my maternal grandmother's house. My children called her Grammy. She was the love of my life. She used to sing to us "You are my Sunshine." She was loved by everyone: but especially by my children and me. I would get to escape with her when I was a child, go on trips with just her and me. We would visit my Great "Granny Goose" Rose Amelia and my (second) cousin David who had Muscular Dystrophy. He was such a sweet soul.

One of the gifts I received from my grandmother was what love wasn't. Having been with my grandfather in an unloving relationship towards the end years. I was by her side as much as I could possibly be. She loved my kids so much, with all her heart. So much so I put a photo of them in her casket. I took care to make sure she went out looking fabulous. She passed of a broken heart. In my opinion, she too had a broken marriage.... this part of the story is to be continued. On the day of the funeral, I did her makeup and her hair. I had "friends" who thought I was morbid, but I didn't think so, I knew how she liked it. I spoiled her by taking her to hair appointments and doing her nails, so I knew. I wanted her to be remembered as she always was: A bright star singing, dancing and laughing. To remember her as someone so full of love and with a big heart. She just wanted to be loved back. I wanted everyone to see that, and not the figure I had to view at the time of her death. I was so angry after she passed away! I felt like she left us... she abandoned me. The day she passed was one of the saddest days of my life. I lost my best friend. That same day the doctors called us in after her surgery had gone horribly wrong. There she lay, hair a mess, her teeth were out and on the table beside her. Her mouth was wide open. I turned and screamed at the nurses. Why had they not made her a bit more presentable? It did not feel real. For God sake, that was not her! Not the Grammy they admitted just two days prior. She was lifeless and stiff. I don't think I have cried as much as I am crying now as I type this out. Snot-nosed and all...I hate this memory.

So for her, I did her makeup and curled her hair, made her as beautiful as I remembered her. Nails all done, embracing a photo of her great-grandchildren, in her favorite outfit. Sending her off to the blue, to heal her broken heart. It was time to say goodbye...In Silent Lucidity. Every time I hear that song, I know it's her saying "hello." I haven't heard that song in a long while, or am I listening? When I would hear that song, I knew that she was around, watching over me, helping me see things through, and protecting me in the night. She's come to me in several different ways. She gave herself so that I could know and find another love, to replace her. She allowed me to run to the "place called home." She's left me shiny things to find after she went to her "place called home."

*In loving memory of my grandmother Lorraine.*

*She's in her place called home*

*Thank you for the gift of unconditional love*

# Chapter Three

## World Changed From Black and White

The cocaine that I refused to take was just the beginning. Adult supervision and guidance was lacking at this time. I was handed drugs and alcohol at the age of fourteen by the vessel virgin, the one that I claim had me by Immaculate Conception, the sinless acts of the virgin. She handed me an envelope with cocaine in it, I refused it. The envelope was wet, and the cocaine had melted. She looked at me and said, "Oh my goodness, here, I'll just eat it." What a good role model. She ate it, paper and all, down the hatch. It was only the beginning of my early drug and alcohol use. I had been offered pot, and on occasion LSD for babysitting the vessel's gal pals' children. Calm down, I never took it while babysitting, I was responsible. I know how to parent, I learned that at the age of nine.

One night I dropped acid with the vessel (probably not the best decision), but I wasn't making good decisions anyway, so chalk it up, lesson learned. While I was sitting there listening to the vessel's ramblings on about her life and sadness--which I could hardly pay attention to--she seemingly thought it was a good idea to talk about it. It was the trip. I get it. I looked over at her, and she began to turn into the wicked witch of the west.

What was at first black and white was now full-on Technicolor. She morphed into the green witch, wart and all. At this point, I was not hearing the words come out of her mouth. Her face began to melt, that is, her tears were melting her face, dripping, like green candle wax. I think about this today, and it was a sad moment and weird moment, one that sticks with me.

I don't know why I haven't forgotten about this, maybe there is more to the story. The witch wasn't wicked. She was sad and had her own negative moments from her past to work out. Was it that her tears were so fierce that she melted or was it that those feeling were being washed away? Was that too deep? Okay, let's get on with the rest of this chapter. She can write her own book.

I recall one day being at a friend's house, we had learned to "huff" paint remover. Oh, the things I could see, life wasn't so black and white anymore...the trip I had. I swear there were aliens and spaceships outside the window as I sat stooped low under the sill, staring out at the sky for hours, at least it seemed like hours. I came to enjoy these trips, away from home, my unsupervised home. I am quite surprised at the genius I am today from my years of drug and alcohol use. They just seemed to open my conscious young mind ever so slightly.

I was hiding behind the drugs, but from what? The adult nurturing figure that I lived with? Maybe. Perhaps it was the horror of everyday life and the revolving door of men and drugged out hippies that passed through the house. Or from roommates who drove ice cream trucks around children's parks higher than a kite. Or maybe from boyfriends who would not allow me to touch their stereo that took up the entire living room. Or another one that came over with garbage bags full of bud.

It was a different time back then, yes the 80s were living. The vessel had gone on a trip to Mexico after the divorce and the sale of our house on Home Street. She left in a VW van full of hippies and my two younger sisters, those poor girls. I had a concert and school dance to attend and refused to go along. They were gone for a month, driving around Mexico while I stayed with a friend and her family. When they arrived back home, they brought with them an even larger VW busload of "tourists." Like the old man used to say: "You can bullshit the tourist, but don't bullshit the natives."

The "tourists" consisted of a young German guy and a couple. The German guy's name was Froggy, and he sure knew how to roll a joint. He taught me how to roll a mean one too. You know, a kid needs skills to survive the jungle. Froggy had a heavy German accent. We could hardly understand him, especially when he was stoned.

Carrie was one-half of the couple. She was a very sweet person. Poor Carrie, her boyfriend seemed nice enough until that one day. I was walking home one evening from my friend's house, came to the house, and walked in the door. Walls full of blood greeted me. There was blood everywhere... it was like a horror movie or a slaughterhouse. Carrie was nowhere to be found, and neither was her boyfriend whom shall go unnamed. Bastard! Carrie had been taken to the hospital. She had been badly beaten, and I am surprised she survived.

I do not recall seeing her again after that, nor do I know what actually happened. I was rushed back off to my friend's house for the night. I do know she was okay, the last I heard. And safe from this animal that was invited into our home. Froggy stuck around for a while after that. The ice cream man stayed. It was a house of cards for sure. Cards and characters. It was a revolving door into the house of mirrors in full living color.

Such is life. We ended up with two rental homes within three blocks of each other. One house for us kids and was a run-down, older home. The other was to grow weed in. It was also a place for the adults to adult. All of this came after my parents' divorce. The house on Home Street sold. The money received from selling the house went to pay in part for the Mexico trip. I try not to judge--she needed it--she needed to spread her wings and experience some of the life she missed. She grew up too fast as well. She was a free spirit wanting to be free.

Sometimes I just find it hard to think of her as my mother back then, after the divorce. I think of her as just the vessel that brought me into this world. I raised myself. I was placed in her womb and birthed, are we all not? I was planted with the seed of my father who art in heaven. I asked to come into this world in this way. I choose my path, my destiny. I made my agreements before coming into this world, and all of this is a part of that. I have co-creators. The vessel nourished me while I was a young whippersnapper. I was taught right from wrong when it should have been love and fear. I grew up quickly. I have been through stuff, lots of stuff. I learned by observation and watching the behavior of others. I had to try some things on to see how they fit. I was good, and I was terrible. I certainly wasn't raised in a Buddhist temple.

I moved out on my own at the age of fifteen and was emancipated at sixteen with the vessels permission. I moved out with a boyfriend to a land far, far away. I moved to Northern California. There I worked two jobs, went to high school and cosmetology school. My younger sisters ended up moving in with the old man since he thought that would be best. The vessel headed out into the wild blue yonder, her free spirit and all. In case you are wondering about what is meant by this, it was a bar the vessel habitually visited. Her group of friends was not allowed inside, so they danced outside in the parking lot. They call themselves "The Frogs."

Now I am going to back up a little and journey back to when I was six years old. On Sundays, my mom would send me out on a bus to the neighborhood Baptist church. The preacher used to slam his fists and preach about hell and damnation, along with fire and brimstone. I was not having this at all. I had been to several churches as a child. I never understood religion, never fit into any one of them. I had been to Catholic, Pentecostal, and Episcopalian churches. You name it; I think I went a time or two. I had no clue what any of these churches had to do with me. I prayed, he answered. Why do I need religion? I have a relationship with God. I have been praying most all my life, or was it just wishful thinking?

As far as I can remember it was working for me. Depending on what I wished for. It didn't always work out the way I intended. I was still learning. Learning how to use my words. Nothing religion said was what my internal dialog had spoken to me. Yes, I would, and still do pick up bits and pieces here and there from ancient texts. However, my inner dialog speaks to me differently. It speaks of love and always gives me hope and inner wisdom. I am not ashamed of "living in sin," having moved out of the house at the age of fifteen. Hell, I don't even believe in sin or confessing it. It was probably the better choice to make considering the circumstances. I did, after all, pray for a better life. Not a good one, but a better one. Words have power, and I am learning this power.

At the age of six, I attended a family wedding in Sebastopol, California. The weddings officiate, whom I shall call Herb, presided over my second cousin's ceremony became a really big part of my life.

I have had a few of these types of people, angels of sorts, enter into my life to teach me my lessons or show me the path I should be on. I had agreements with them to come into my life before I was born. The contracts no longer serve my purpose, but they are never forgotten. Somehow, Herb and I just connected. He was an older gentleman, and it turns out we shared the same birthday. We ended up becoming pen pals for years. That's what we did back in the old days; we actually exchanged letters using snail mail. They came to the San Joaquin Valley to visit me when I was about eleven years old. His wife came along, and we talked about current events, well the events of an eleven-year-old. I used to get packages from him, prayers, and a bookmark. I still have the bookmark this day, and it reads:

*O Lord, help my words to be gracious and tender, for tomorrow I may have to eat them.*

My friendship with the Herb seemed unconditional. I cherished our relationship as pen pals. We wrote to each other at least once a month--until the day things changed. I had been writing to him about my boyfriend and me moving in together. He had probably always pictured me as a sweet girl, which I was. However, I lost my virginity very young, at around the age of fourteen.

At the time of our falling out, I was fifteen, and I was moving out into the big world on my own. According to Herb, I was a sinner because my boyfriend was eighteen and I was fifteen.

We were in love. HA! I received a letter back from Herb, it turned out that he was totally disgusted with me. He explained that this was unacceptable and he would never write to me again. We never communicated again after that. That was the end of what I thought was an unconditional friendship, being a good Christian and all.

In his world, I was going to be living in sin, and he did not condone this. Ties were cut, and our friendship was over. He would never write to me again. When I look back on this, I sometimes wish the vessel would have stopped me from moving out. Sometimes I wish she had put her foot down. That if she had, things would have been different. Do I really believe that? No, I don't. I know I must go through my life this way. I know I had to learn disappointment and to find love. I know I had to find my God connection.

I am not trying to blame anyone for my upbringing. I had good times as well. I learned to be an adult at a young age and to fend for myself. I see such experiences being all part of my journey, my agreements, and my contracts for this current life path; my path to Love.

Paths cross, people meet all the time. I see the signs, all the time. This having come full circle for me. I now live and create in Sebastopol, California. I am now looking for any shred of Herb's existence so I can say my peace, so I can forgive and let this chapter go. I need to find the color and the light in the dark places of my memory of him, so I may find solace and feel a bit lighter. I need to drop this baggage off at the grave of abandonment, yet again.

*Some journeys take us far from home,*

*Some adventures lead us to our destiny*

*-CS Lewis*

*In loving memory of Herb*

*There truly is no sin, but I am sure you know that*

*now*

*Love is the color of my world*

*Green is the color of Love*

*Thank you for the gifts*

# Chapter Four

## Where Is This Un-Named God?

Now I am a twenty-one-year-old woman. I am living with my baby daddy and my small child of about four months old. I am having thoughts on getting married and having more children. Our child was born out of wedlock. I dream of a happy married life, raising the kids. You know, the nice house, white picket fence thing. My fantasies involve living on a small farm with a bit of livestock and a garden. That is my dream.

Instead, what I have is an angry, drunk of a man who came from an angry drunk of a father and an abused mother. I am in need of one thing: unconditional love. What else does anyone need? Unconditional love, the kind of love I have for my baby girl. The kind of love you get from a good childhood, nurturing parents, or a supportive friend that grew up in the old neighborhood. A friend that wants to have a girl's night out to catch up on life because we hadn't seen each other in seven or more years. The kind of supporting love where your boyfriend says "Sure, have a great time, I will go have poker night with the guys." That kind of trusting love.

What a girl needs is the kind of love that makes her heart center vibrate. She needs the kind of love that I received from my grandmother because my grandmother knew she wanted that kind of love too. He was going to head out and enjoy an evening with his buddies playing poker. It was a good night, hanging out with my good friend, catching up on old times. She was telling me about college, and I was chatting about my new job as a nail technician. Talking about my baby girl and all the new stuff she could do. I was having a good time.

He had arrived home just minutes before myself. Things might have been different if it had been the other way, although it is highly doubtful. Nothing made sense one way or the other. I had a great time and was excited to hear about his night. I was ready to share a good time. I was greeted at the door . . . only to meet my worst fear.

As I was walking into the apartment, I was greeted with a fist to the face, another to the side of my head. No questions were asked, and no words were spoken. There was one punch in the gut and few more to the face for good measure. Oh, it was getting good now, maybe I deserved this, I thought.

I had too good of a time. Perhaps a punch to the gut and a few more was what was needed just to teach me my lesson. The fear had reached into my gut, that is, the fear that nobody was going to save me, not even God. I was screaming for help, but not even God could help me. I was thrown to the ground and tried to fight him off. I rolled into the fetal position. I had no strength. The kicks just kept coming until I just could not take it any longer and passed out. I recall screaming for help a few times with whatever breath I had. Not even God could hear me. Not one soul through the thin-walled apartment complex heeded my call. But where is GOD? Why was nobody listening?

It was a knock-out! The morning sun was rising and peeking through the blinds. As I am waking up from a good night's rest, I thought it was all just a bad dream because he was gone. He had left for work. Maybe this didn't actually happen. Maybe I had a bit too much to drink, and it was a nightmare. I move slightly and there it is. I writhe in pain. I manage to get myself to the bathroom, and my biggest fear appears in the mirror. There is a monster looking back at me. Hysterically, I try to recognize this person as I begin to cry. What happened? Did this really happen? I start sobbing uncontrollably. I can't stop. My face is blown up like a balloon in black, blue, purple, and green. All I can think about is my daughter, where is she? The phone rings. I manage to control the sobbing. I answer it. It's his mother: "Bernie is bringing Rose home this morning, he is on his way." I just need my baby girl to hold and love, I must compose myself. Finally, a knock on the door, maybe it is someone to help me or had heard me yelling for help the night before, and they wanted to see if I was okay, now that the coast was clear. Someone now able to see this monster he made me. I go to answer the door, fearful of what everyone outside might see. I must have deserved this, I was out late, and I had a good time. It's my baby and her Pop-Pop, surely he will see me and help me. I go to reach for her, shaking and in much pain. She barely recognizes me and has a look of confusion. I reach out and hold her reassuring her I am her mommy and everything will be okay. You can't mistake a mother's love. Bernie stands there, not a peep, not a feeling, no expressions, not even a helping hand or a question. Only a "well okay, see you later." My guess is he didn't want to get involved.

Now this was a full circle from one father to another. You see, his father did the same thing to his mother, as the old man did to the vessel. I don't know why I thought this was a good relationship. We met on a blind date. He took a liking to me. I tried to turn it into love. I had been taken many times against my will when he was drunk. Even when I made it very clear that I was out of birth control pills, I ended up with child. We were doing the right thing by staying together and getting married, even though he didn't really love me. Why had God put me here? Why this vicious circle? Where was my "voice," my answers? After all of this, I received an apology. Was it sincere? No. Would he do it again? Yes! He had done it before, while I was pregnant. It was not as bad as this time. This was the worst. He told me how much he loved me. How fucking belittling! But I forgave him anyway. We got married just two months later, had another child two years later. Was this some kind of karma? Was this our past life revenge? He hated me.

My two children are beautiful and loving. I see God in them. They remind me of God's miracles. I am blessed. I have forgiven, and have let all this go. I used to say there was only one person in the world I have hatred for and it was him, but something inside made me forgive. I have known my inner voice for as long as I can remember. I also keep all of my vivid memories. This one needs to go, it needs to be healed. By telling this part of my story, I know it will be. There is a lesson in this memory, from a past life. The story of abuse by my first husband, my children's father. Looking back, I have forgiven him and released the anger many years ago. He has since passed away. He left this earth and is now stuck in the ether somewhere, being taught how to receive love, and not try to take it by force or with control because you didn't get your way in one life or another. It was his agreement too. One day he will be free. Hopefully his father Bernie is now with him, guiding him. Bernie has passed too. He passed by the hand of his wife, a hand that was also a part of my story of abuse. She laid a hand upon him, and now he is gone.

I truly believe he was taken to show his son the way back to love. His father did stop the beating and drinking long before I met them. He really did try to make up for his mistakes, maybe just not hard enough. Not long ago I had a dream that my ex was standing at the foot of my bed, he reached out to hug me and said he loved me and that he was sorry. Incidentally, this happened right after his passing. So, I received a gift: the gift of forgiveness. He still has some making up to do, not with me, but to himself.

I know in a past life I abandoned him, but for reasons born out of love. He was still angry with me for this. He showed me in the only way he knew how. The only way he was taught, by his own parents. I accepted this contract, but only for a short while. My daughter also had a dream, only of her Pop-Pop recently. He came to her and gave her a hug. In the dream, she went to find her brother, but when she came back with her brother, Pop-Pop was gone. He still has work to do. He will return when he is done, in my son's dreams. I believe their gift will one day be for both father and Pop-Pop to enter into my children's dreams and hug them both so they can be forgiven and heal as well. My children will heal, we all do before returning home.

*In accepting and forgiving memory of Kirk*

*Thank you for the gifts*

*They are both beautiful and full of Love*

*Thank you, I get to live with that.*

*God awaits your return.*


*In Loving memory of Bernie*

*Take care of your son*

*Don't abandon his love.*

*Know your grandchildren adored you*

SAINT MICHAEL
PROTECT US

# Chapter Five

## The Father, The Son, and Holy Shit

I sometimes feel as if I was born with all the knowledge of

the universe. I am a natural born expert in everything. I believe that

a child is born with all the knowledge of the universe. This is not a

new idea, of course. For example, the philosophers Plato and

Descartes supported the view that we are born knowing, a view

known as Innatism. From this view, we are born with innate

knowledge of our soul, our world. It is society and the people that

surround us that changes us. We are changed by our environment,

our parents, our friends, our elders, and what we learn from them.

We all have this inner knowing, wisdom, and intuition, they are

our gifts. For example, I can remember parts of my life back to the

age of two. I can recall feeling as if I did not belong because of this

innate knowing. For me, this was especially true knowing that the

old man who raised me was not my biological father.

On a day like any other, my parents divorced. On this

particular day, when I was thirteen, we packed up our belongings

and moved out of the Home Street house. That same day I

happened upon a photo of my co-creator, the seed of my existence in human form. Oh, father where art thou? Somehow God had pointed me in the direction to find and look into my baby book. In it was a picture of a rebel without a cause, an Aidan Quinn look-alike. I went to the vessel with the photo and asked who this person was as if I didn't already know the answer. I was seeking and needing confirmation.

This photo had three people in it, but I was particularly interested in only one. My father. The vessel looks at me and says, "Oh, that's your father and your grandparents." My reaction was priceless. I said back to her, "WELL THEN . . . WHO THE FUCK IS THAT GUY?" I was speaking of the old man that I called dad for the first twelve years of my life, that guy that she was now divorcing. Who was the old man that has been in my life since I was eight months old? I somehow knew they would eventually divorce. I was actually happy they were divorcing. The fights and drunkenness, I was glad it was going to be over. Life could only get better.

That day I had a sense that something was beginning to unravel and that my life would change forever. I began to move into another phase of life. That was the day I became an aggressive investigator, a natural born expert in everything. I am not claiming to be a scholar. I have taken courses and researched and read anything that spirit has pointed me to. I have read the signs, the writings on the wall as it were. I listened to the voice's direction, directing me like a professor in my mind. I did not even graduate high school. Mind you, I am fine with this because I possess an innate knowing and wisdom. I believe in universal laws that require no formal education. These are the laws of cause and effect. I am reminded that some of the most creative and intelligent people did not have proper schooling. It has worked out just fine for me, on my path, and for that I am proud.

Recently, I have put my investigating hat on and found several family members I was not aware of at the time. I love ancestry and genealogy. It took me thirty years, but I have found my two older sisters, several cousins, and two aunts. All others I managed to track down have since passed on. I am fortunate to have opened up that gift, and I am still unwrapping it.

My interest in genealogy comes from my Great Aunt Selma, my grandmother's sister. She and my grandmother passed down that gene along with a lot of family records. I have made new connections with family over the years. I found what had been lost after the matriarchs left us. I am grateful for my Great Aunt who had much to do with the family search division of the Latter Day Saints. I was fortunate enough to finally find and visit my father's gravesite, put to rest alongside his parents, my grandparents. He died young... a skydiver for fun. He perished in a plane crash. He was my guide in the heavens.

Although he did not know me while he was alive, I know he does now. He watched me as I grew up. He kept me safe--although I was not always sane--with a watchful eye. He was hanging out with my grandmother and the gang (she was a very flirty lady). For the last thirty years, I have had this sense that he has been unconditionally guiding me to find my family. I have this sense that he and my grandmother teamed up: my best friend and the father. They never judge my decisions or me. Well, there was that one time: Grammy judged my butt. This was more of a warning maybe. She patted my behind and said, "better watch that, big butts run in the family." I took it as a compliment. One time my two-year-old lifted my maternity dress and said to me, "mommy, you have a big ass butt." Out of the mouth of babes. Learned by the mouth of her father.

Soon after my ex-husband passed, he came to me in a dream. When I woke the next morning, I felt like a huge weight had been lifted. I felt lighter. You see, he passed from his addictions. He died as a result of his abuse of alcohol and prescription pills. Ironically, these were the same pills that were intended to kill the pain from his waist down, but he really needed them to kill the pain from the waist up.

One afternoon I was waiting for him to return home with diapers and formula for my youngest son. My sweet little boy was just seven months old at the time, and my little girl was three. What was taking so long? He hadn't returned home yet from work, and I was getting frantic because I was quickly running out of supplies for the babies. I knew that he was probably going to come home drunk again.

We were living with his parents because we had been evicted from our apartment, again. I called the bar he frequented after work, and as usual, they lied. "He left" was the reply. More time passed, and he still wasn't home. I called the bar again, this time I think they sensed worry in my tone. They confirmed that he had left the bar. My gut was telling me something wasn't right, so I packed the kids in the car as I was internally guided to drive his normal route home. When I drove up to that one curve in the road, the one by the Chevron station, I saw police and an ambulance leaving the scene. There remained his wrecked motorcycle and one work boot. How ironic, when they searched for my father's body in the lake the plane crashed in, all they found was his foot, in his boot.

I knew, I just knew. I screamed out the window of my car trying to retrieve information on the who, what, and where of what happened. It turned out that he had been transported to the hospital so I drove back to his parent's house and I called the bar. Why had they let him drink so much? Boy did I let them have it!

Through all the Xanax for me and some rehabilitation and jail time for him, he came out of this the same asshole he had been in the first place. I was so stupid to think this would change him. Despite this, I stayed with him for another three years. The only difference was that he was now paraplegic. His disability had not changed him, not one fucking bit. He was even angrier than he was before and deep down I knew he wouldn't change. I'll stay for the kids I thought. I'll wait it out. Ha! What a joke.

He was good with the kids, the first four years of being together. However, at some point, he started picking on our son. He wanted to make him a man. He was still a baby! It was mostly verbal abuse, he was really good at that. Strange enough, his parents adored the kids and really did a lot for them and for that I am grateful.

He still came after me too. He came after me the broomstick, tree branches, and the usual abusive words. His words hurt just as much if not more. I also noticed him starting to get angrier with the kids. He started drinking more and mixing his drinking with prescription pills. Emotionally, he couldn't handle his disability and often wondered why this was happening to him. He used to bang on the side of the house when he needed something outside in the garage, yelling for the kids to bring him something.

Around this time, my grandmother, my best friend, passed away. She was my children's beloved Grammy. She lived alone at her "place called home" now. The house I had known all my life, the house she bought when I was just a baby. My grandfather had passed about a year before. Before her passing, they really didn't have much of a relationship

left. They lived in different cities and had grown apart in heart and illness. She had turned to his younger brother because he had always been in love with her. He told me about his love for her but lamented that he couldn't be with her.

The two of them had a cute little affair going. Prior to my grandfather passing, my great uncle would come up to the valley during the winters and stay with both of them and continued to do so after my grandfather passed. I think that was the happiest she had been in a long time.

Around midnight one night, I got a call. It was my great uncle. They had taken her to the hospital by ambulance he said. I rushed over to the hospital as quickly as I could. A couple of days later, after needing surgery, she passed. I always say she died of a

broken heart. That day it started to sink in: not only had my best

friend passed, but I refused to live like or die like this. During the

last decade of her life, she did not live a happy life with my

grandfather. At that time he moved out, after accusing her of

poisoning him. I was and am worthy of so much more! I needed

more than what I was receiving.

It wasn't long after that day in January. The vessel was

living in my grandmother's house while things got sorted out.

Springtime, the rodeo, and my sister's birthday came. This was one

of the best times I had in a long time. Men were hitting on me,

complimenting me. I had not been out in a very long time. I could

sense that I could be loved. The gray gloom that I had been stuck

in was suddenly lifted, and I was a fucking ray of sunshine. I could

sense my groove coming back. They were asking for my phone

number . . . but I couldn't. I was married, or was it a prison?

I am not sure what happened next, but I think I can say that

he probably could see that my spirits had been lifted, and my

sunshine was beginning to appear. I had actually been pondering the thought of leaving him. Yes, it sounded really good. I came home from work the next day, the kids were at their Nana's. He was angry at something, probably because I brought home some sunshine. He kept taunting me, probing me with a broom handle. This time it was different. I stood my ground, I really stood my ground. I was like a bull. He kept taunting, yelling, and coming towards me with that stick. I went for the phone to call 911 but he yanked the cord from the wall. It was a good thing his mother was on her way to drop the kids off. She could hear yelling as she pulled into the driveway and decided it best to leave the kids in the car as she proceeded to walk into the house.

When she walked in, I was foaming at the mouth mad. I yelled at her to put the kids in my car NOW! I screamed at him. "THAT'S FUCKING IT!" I grabbed the stick from his hand, rammed it into the spokes of his wheelchair and screamed: "I HAVE HAD IT!" His mother stopped in her footsteps, jaw to the ground. I fucking let him have it. I hit him in the head, punched him in the face, and knocked him right out of his chair while screaming at him "FUCK YOU, FUCK YOU, FUCK YOU!" His mother stood frozen in her tracks, and she finally yelled to me,

"Just run and get the kids and go." I think she had a flashback. I had to try to compose myself a bit, assured my children everything was fine as we drove off to Grammy's house. We stayed there for quite some time. I was home, the only home where I have ever felt truly safe.

*Thank you Grammy for the sacrifice, and for being a home to always come home to, even in your passing*

*This was a great gift, thank you for always being there for me, even in your passing*

*Thank you for the gift that opened my eyes and set me free*

*333*

# Chapter Six

# Locked Up Soul

There was a day that my son's father took him out of school early. Not both children, just one. He wasn't supposed to do this sort of thing without first consulting with me, without mutual consent. Things were still rough between us. I had spun out a little in life a few years before and after our separation. As if things weren't bad enough, I had had two DUIs and was working on getting my shit together. I was a little scared of what might be happening and why he took my son out of school knowing very well that I would be picking him up.

This part of my story is a little bit about angels watching over me. At the time, I was living with the man I am still married to today, my "now" husband. I was pacing and fuming because the ex had our son. I needed to pick him up and get an explanation. My "now" husband didn't think it was a good idea and in hindsight, he was probably right. But it wasn't a good idea for the ex to pick him up either. What was he up to? It wasn't his visitation day.

I drove to his house to find out what was going on and to pick up my son. I drove up, and he was outside in his wheelchair with my son waiting for me. We began bantering back and forth. Then the police drove up and parked behind my car. I got a strange feeling in my gut. Why were they here? I had no idea. I was within my parental rights. Did he know something I didn't? I could not comprehend why this evil son of a bitch always got away with everything he did. Was it karma? I think it was just vengeance. Maybe it was his way of still trying to control me.

I approached the officers to ask them why they were here, there was really no legitimate reason. I had custody papers with me and could present them to the officers. They asked for my ID, but why mine? What was this asshole up to? I was clearly within my parental rights. Then it occurred to me. It flashed before my eyes. He must have found out about my outstanding warrant and planned this attack. He was still angry that I left him and that I was happy to have custody of the children. He knew how I felt about him as an angry drunk, a woman beater, and that he managed to get himself paralyzed. He was getting back at me. Somehow he found out about this warrant for a past DUI that I was still working on taking care of once I quit digging myself into holes. I was arrested and put in handcuffs right in front of my six-year-old.

I got this DUI in Santa Clara County where I went to a beauty show. Back then I was in the Beauty Biz, I was a nail technician. I got a little buzzed while I was there. I couldn't afford to stay the night like the others decided to do, so I decided to drive home back to the valley. I got in the car and got on the freeway. I was driving fine. I was talking on my cell phone (the big brick ones from the 90s), and I dropped it on the floor. I went to retrieve it and swerved a bit. The lights went on, and they pulled me over. I passed the roadside tests just fine. However, they needed to give me a Breathalyzer test. I think I blew a .081. That was it. Book'em Danno. I could not afford to fight it, I pleaded. I couldn't afford to pay the fines. I received a DUI and then a warrant.

Now I sit in the back of the black and white, driving off as my son watches, the both of us in tears. I was about to take an all-expense paid trip into the California Jail System. The next three weeks were the longest of my life. I prayed and prayed they would just let me go but there was no way, this was my hell. This was also a lesson in Angels. I believe I was sent one. She was with me until the City of Angels. One girl, one big beautiful dark lady, was sent to see me through and to protect me.

I was skinny, white, and scared. This angel, she sat with me the whole time, stood up for me when harassed, and protected me. My prayers were heard: not of letting me go, but keeping me safe so I could make it home in one piece. We were packed onto a bus and ready to hit the road. We were shackled at the ankles and the wrists inside cages. This was, we were told, to keep us safe from the male criminals in the back of the bus. Mind you, they were not in cages, tight cages, like we were. We stopped at every small town jail dropping off and picking up prisoners. My angel was beside me the whole way, letting me know we were okay. I was terrified, shaking in my cuffs and my big girl panties.

We arrived in Los Angeles where we were to stay overnight before heading up to Northern California, where I had to be transported back to Santa Clara County. This was my tour of the beautiful golden state and also where I got separated from my angel. We had a stopover at the Sybil Brand Institute. This place was creepy. There were a lot of women there. We were put into an all-purpose room with bunks three high, side by side. I picked the highest one, and I stayed there. Many of these women were prostitutes and drug addicts. Many were coming down off of heroin. We were given green bologna sandwiches to eat or use as pillows. Not a hard choice to make, I would take hunger over a place to lay my head.

Another angel showed up. This time she sat across from my bunk, on the third one as well. I liked it up there because this way we could see what was going on around us. It turned out that this woman was a Yoga instructor. What on earth was a Yoga instructor doing in a women's prison? I didn't dare ask. All I knew was that she was comforting to me and that we practiced bunk Yoga breathing.

Days passed, and I began to worry. Why? Had they forgotten I was traveling? Had my ship left? I later learned that they did forget about me but eventually did put me back on a North-bound bus. We stopped at all the famous places on the way, picking up and dropping off prisoners. Wasco, Salinas, Avenal, Corcoran, and San Quentin. The last stop was mine: Santa Clara

County. This place was a cake walk compared to what I had just gone through. We had single bunks, a library with seating, and we were free to roam. There was an outside area, a smoking area and we could even get acupuncture if we wanted. This place was a spa compared to the nightmare I went through to get there.

After fighting with the old man on the phone and getting absolutely no help from the vessel, my "now" husband came to my rescue. He lovingly pawned his motorcycle to rescue me from my now three-week nightmare tour of California. I said my goodbyes, left all my things behind and got the hell out of that place.

Women can be so mean. Not one person gifted me a smoke or talked to me. I thank goodness for my angels getting me through the toughest parts. I left a little note in one of the books in the library. The note mentioned that how shameful it was for women to treat one another the way these women did here. I signed it LOVE JESUS. Mr. Now never did get that motorcycle out of pawn, but we ended up purchasing two more since that time. I forced him to. I went back home as if I was away in college and thanked my angels and said my prayers so that I would never return. Mr. Now's friends tried to warn him not to pawn his bike, I was not worth it. Our song at the time was; If You Could Only See.

*Much love and gratitude to you Mr. Now*

*You get me! I love you with all my heart and soul!*

# Chapter Seven

# My Opinions and The Animals

The Universe spoke to me in a whisper, asking me to share my innermost secrets, struggles, tools, and gifts. I was asked to share my vibrational energy. I remember when I received the message, and it was quite clear. The memory has stuck with me all these years. I have long had dreams of building a holistic healing empire of creating a line of herbal products. I have had dreams of opening my own Holistic Health Healing Center. All of my dreams were driven by my need to reach out to others. That all changed when I was awakened by the whisper.

When it began to be more crystal clear to me, the whisper told me that I must write my stories in the form of a book in order to share my gifts. I was told to put them to paper and send them out into the commonality. This may seem weird I know, but I am weird. When I first heard the whisper, parts of my story were still in the process of being created because I was living them.

I recently received a new message. It pointed me to write my first book. So here we are. I was to write this for the survivors of the world, for the warriors, the seekers: YOU. By reading my pages, you will hopefully move on to find your own stories to tell and create your new experience as a gift to the world. By telling our stories we release the baggage that holds us back, and we begin to learn to create a new story. We learn to visualize a new way of life. This story is to continue on these pages, so please keep reading as I now share "my opinions," and who they are. I want to share how animals, survival skills, and life's magic have all helped me. I am putting what God gave me up for sale. I have been given the green light to move forward. I hope to touch you in some way that one day you can share your story openly with others. Create your new life and let the past go. Realize that we are all one creation needing to connect on higher vibrations to bring some peace to Mother Earth as the divine souls that we are.

I don't remember much of what I wrote in my diaries as a child. I believe it was mostly stuff like what the day had involved and my wishes or dreams at the time. I do remember writing down experiences I had that bring meaning to my current self. That is the significant stuff that has shaped me and who I am today. The intentions I wrote then were goals for the future. I write and speak in many different styles. "I AM" is now. Spells are affirmations or prayers. My imagination has always served me as an escape as well as a prison. I AM always creating new ways to create my new life.

Writing down my thoughts has always been about what I love and what I have feared. It's about writing down your internal voice and the feelings vibrating from your heart. It's about releasing old patterns and finding our souls through ascension. I really started journaling again in my early thirties out of a pure intention to keep me sane. In my twenties I kept my thoughts and feeling up in my head, battling back and forth, neglecting to put pen to paper. At that time I had lost the desire to connect. I had felt that God didn't care. I was just bottling it all up, feeding the fears. I had no way to release those feelings. I was looking for love in all the wrong places.

I began learning again how to set my intentions, present my wishes, and let go of the anger or confusion in those early journals. Sometime in my late twenties, I began consciously writing again. This was when I began communicating with Gladys and My Opinions. Some call what I began doing automatic writing. You can call it whatever you like. I still have many of these early journals. I also wrote in old-school style notepads; however, those no longer exist after having moved so many times. They got thrown out, burned, or lost. It doesn't matter because the universe holds them. It was a way to leave my thoughts, my wishes, my prayers to the universe to answer through Gladys or the others in My Opinions.

Gladys was always there for me and for the most part, answered my questions. She was sweet and endearing. I continue to give much love and gratitude to God every day for these gifts. I don't know where I would be if I hadn't made the simple choice to write out what I was feeling, what I wanted to happen in my life. Yes, there were times when I felt hope had been lost. In those moments I wrote even more. I was angry as to why these things and events were happening to me. Was it because I had stopped listening? Who was to blame for all the bad things? What karma did I have to make the universe do such things? In the end, it turned out that it wasn't the universe, it was me and my choices. I put myself in those situations. These were my soul contracts and agreements, and I had to learn how to get myself out of them, through them.

At the time of my connection with Gladys and My Opinions, the vessel began to connect with me as more of an adult and a mother. She amazingly decided to begin nourishing my gifts. She would send me crystals and small holistic items. She sent me my first deck of divining cards: my Animal Medicine Card deck. I still have them to this day and turn to them for my consulting work with others as well as for myself. I have always looked to these totem animals for their omens and signs. These are little messages from the universe in daily life.

Between the ages of twenty-six and thirty were not easy years for me. I went through an ugly separation and divorce. I also suffered the loss of my granddad, grandmother, and great-uncle. They were kind of the trinity of old folks that the helped keep me going in my teens and twenties. When I needed something one of them was always there. They were there to pick me up, help me pack, and move me out when I needed it. Grammy slipped me money when my granddad wasn't looking because she embezzled from herself, and I found this hilarious. They would pay me way too much money for a home pedicure, and they tipped me well. They were my stability, my guiding lights, and my sunshine when the vessel was not available. The vessel was offline... She was still finding herself. At this time in my life, I dated very little and worked several small jobs to make ends meet. I went through a couple of boyfriends/roommates and did some unmentionables back in those days . . . but those stories are for another book. They don't call it the dirty thirties for nothin'.

This was also another time when I started using drugs and alcohol. I managed these habits only when my children were with their father on visitation. I AM a good mom. I was riding the rails, doing the nails, cocktail waitress by night, and part-time receptionist in the morning. I was re-connecting with my lost youth. The divorce party was on, and I would try to make up for lost time. I grew up too fast. I thought I deserved to party, to go out and stay up half the night. The rails gave me the energy to move on. They gave me sexual energy, and they also got me in touch with My Opinions and higher sub-conscious. This was a part of my Emerald path. On the path I came across a hole and stepped into it.

I was halfway in and halfway out. Then, finally down the hole, I went. This was the time I also found love.

Automatic writing and channeling were and still are my thing. I didn't need to go to therapy for my problems. I despised therapy. Einstein once said that significant problems cannot be solved at the same level of the thinking that created them. Only by rising to a higher or deeper level can an ultimate solution to psychological problems be found. That is what automatic writing and channeling did for me. It allowed me to reach those higher, deeper levels of my mind. I allowed Spirit to guide me.

By thinking of the thought or question that was happening in my life and writing down the concerns or questions, I began to feel the emotions associated with the question or event. I would visualize and take a step back. I could see myself telling the story. My hand would begin to write a new version or answers to the questions I asked. I would follow my instinct to where Spirit would have me look for the answers and write them down.

As we grow, the negative and unproductive patterns outlive their use. Then as we mature we seek to create new, healthier patterns. It's not that the negative patterns leave, they simply go dormant, and the new healthier patterns take over. We learn, as the old grandfather did, to feed the good wolf. It makes sense to accept this and have compassion for not only the old negative patterns but for the child or young adult who needed them at the time. Only when old patterns that no longer serve us are released can new ones emerge. Sometimes new, healthier habits must be in place before releasing the old ones. That is where I AM at this time. I AM still reaching those higher, deeper astral fields, one step at a time, and one sentence at a time.

Animal Medicine helps in the discovery of our power, a discovery by way of animals and what they intend to teach us. This medicine helps us to get in sync with our conscious mind. This synchronicity needs to be released in order to aid our personal growth. Every part of our creation has a place on the wheel of all that is. For me, it was a process of connecting with mother earth and all viable creatures. It was a doorway of understanding and recognizing my oneness. This divining process along with automatic writing helped me gain my life and path back. I did a reading at least once a week, sometimes even daily. I would pull a card after asking a question. I would begin to write what the card

was asking or telling me at that moment. This was just the gateway

to my gifts. I began to learn more about the great universe and its

total synchronicity.

**From my journals with My Opinion and the Animals**
**APRIL 7TH, 1997**
**My opinion**
*Your old soul is getting older. You're getting tired and weak.*
*Watch your health, you have a long life this time. Don't cry. We*
*are always here for you when others are not. We love you and*
*are here for you. We are watching out for your lighthearted*
*soul. It may not seem like it now my child, but rewards are*
*great. You will have what you need, mind, body, heart, and*
*soul. Hang in there. You do no harm to anyone, we know this,*
*and that's what counts. We love you.*

**Me**

*I feel I'm getting back to the norm, but also being fooled. Then I fear my strengths. I must stay strong and dig out of this hole for the sake of my babies and myself. Keep above water. No one can do it for me, I know that and have been there all too many times. Yeah, everyone cares about me, but I feel that's only as far as it goes. A loving thought or physical action when convenience sees to it. I am supposed to take care of number one and my own first. When will I learn this and not let anyone tell me otherwise ... or am I selfish? They can all be selfish and change the rules to fit. I am human too, am I not? I'm different. So very different it hurts. But the pain slowly lessens. I'll be numb soon. Just myself and my own. The way it should be I guess.*

**My opinion**

*Get over the fear, and be powerful again for you. You must or be miserable.*

Life was my doing because I was not listening to My Opinion. The voice that spoke to me was in all those sheets of paper. It was the voice that was always there for me and told me how things really were. Was I somehow not getting the message? I was looking for another path. My path at the time was kind of gray, like a gray, dimly lit street. On that street stood houses, little blue houses. But I did not have the keys. I was stuck in what seemed like a long rainy season, and I lost my keys to the house to which I belonged, searching for signs of life. The life I was meant to live.

**APRIL 8TH, 1997**

**Me**

*Feeling a little better today. I feel blocked. I feel stuck with little creative artistic and move-able freedom. Like I can't create on my own time. I am walking on the time of others. I can't even get that right sometimes. I miss having my home and my family. My new family. My blood family. I also miss "my opinions" living. At least we still communicate huh? I need your help. You know I don't like to ask nor do I like receiving it. But I am asking... HELP. I need so badly to get out of this stagnation and confusion. I need the help of whoever can help me. Please bring me some creative energy and a little funding to help my family move on and so my most lovable mate doesn't have to work so hard. Thank you all who help. I love you.*

**My opinion**

*We will do what we can love. Stick to it. Don't let anything get you down. Keep striving. You are as strong as you are beautiful darling girl. You need some regenerating your energy. Rest a little love. You need it now. Regenerate, and we can help, rest for now doll, we love you.*

That day I did my animal medicine reading, and I pulled the Lizard card. Lizard is dreaming: joining My Opinion in the Dream-time to regenerate my reality. It was telling me that it was time to dream my future, to map my future. It was telling me I needed more sleep and to rest. I needed to regenerate.

Nowadays I don't use the terms Gladys and My Opinions to describe this voice. I say God or angels now. Gladys and My Opinions have moved on. However, I do I miss them because they have shown me the way to God. We all have a way to God. God speaks to us all in many different ways. I am here to share those ways with you so that you may see and feel how he talks to you, teaching you to create the life you are meant to live.

When you learn to let go to that which does not serve you, the magic begins to happen. The puzzles of life become much easier to solve. You begin to find the missing pieces. When you quit working against your ego, your true self-emerges and you can begin to see your own path. I call this book the Emerald Path because love is always green, the color of love. It's like that saying, "the grass isn't always greener on the other side, we just need to water our own lawn." The healing color of green takes that which troubles you and transforms into something beautiful. Green is the color of the heart chakra and relates to love of self. When we are in balance, we are able to give this love, to share the love. My hope, as you read on, is that your heart has opened just a little bit more to your own path.

*APRIL 13TH, 1997*
*Me*
*Thanks again! Positive is just a flowing! Life is a lot rosier now. I feel the new air around myself and my family. Don't wear yourselves out now... I love you*

*My opinion*
*You are so very welcome my dear. All you need is to ask. We will always be here when needed. Keep that smile on your face and the faces of the ones who love you. We are smiling with joy for you and yours love. Goodnight*

That day I pulled the Elk card, the card of Stamina. Elk tells me that I was setting my pace for high mountains. I was becoming the warrior and goddess energy. I was finding my unity or oneness. I was heading to the peaks of LOVE that I deserved. But I had some mountains to climb still. I had to be rid of bad habits to get out of the hole I was about to put myself into. This was the time I said goodbye to drugs. I now know that Gladys and

My Opinions were my elders that had passed on.

*In loving memory of you all*

*My Father, Gladys, and Grammy*

*Thank you for showing up.*

# Chapter Eight

# OM My God

*February 7th, 2017*
*Dear God,*
*You and I have an appointment to meet this afternoon. Please show up, same time, same place.*

*Deep Joy*

*Sing for Joy. OM*

*For God, OM*

*We can do this, shout out loud*

*OM earth beneath*

*Burst into song*

*Your mountains, your forest, and all your trees*

*Bequeath*


There is and always will be a universal calling for each of us to share our stories so that others who are searching for their own divinity may find it and do the same. It's a soul history, a record of finding yourselves. It is like leaving breadcrumbs when you are lost. It is written in the libraries, bookstores, and the

Akashic records for all to access. It is about seeing the symbols and messages at the right time and the right place all around us.

Our paths change, our paths cross, we come to forks in the road, and have to make choices. No, this way, not that way, says the straw-man on the field. There are always so many choices, but generally, it is always two that lead to home. One choice may be a longer and more painful one, the other glorious and less bumpy. The choice to let it be or the choice to fix it. One choice has steered you to read this book.

If you want to find your magic, there are signs everywhere. We can find them in books, in songs, in art, and in our favorite movies or TV shows. Once you open up to journaling, writing, reading, and observing, you will begin to see the magic appear. Open up your heart chakra, your love shack. Take a look deep inside and see what you need to heal. Your soul will begin to shine and sparkle in conversations if you listen to the magic. Really listen.

This will happen if you keep yourself open to receive and don't hide your magic. Be open, be weird with your creative self, with your magic and gifts. Come out of your closets. We can't hear you if you don't speak, write or show yourself. Show it off. Share it. Let your light shine. Don't be afraid of the others who try to shove you back in the box. Open your box, set it free. The world doesn't need more storage, it needs more light. Unpack your baggage at last and stay awhile. Create the path you wish to be on, no matter what color it is. A book, a journal, and pads of paper are lighter loads to carry and store.

Build your castles. Create your dreams. It's all there with the use of your hands and your conscious mind. Your pen pal in the sky is there to help you create and get that ballpoint moving. Without the magic of creating we lose the sense of creating. Creating with words, art, music, your craft, the lives we wish to live, the legacy to keep on living and leave behind for up and coming generations to find. Find your soul again through the creative and imaginative process. There are creative forces that leave breadcrumbs to help us find our souls so that we can unlock our love and joy. Awaken every cell in your body with invisible awareness and energy. Numerologists believe that every name and word vibrates to a dynamic, vital energy. Each number has an associated letter that vibrates to a specific frequency. Each word has power. Harnessing and learning numerology can answer even the very simple questions you have. Everything is connected.

I went through a transformation in my thirtieth year. The year was 1996. I call it my dirty thirty. I was still dealing with the "shopping cart" (that was a nickname a friend gave my ex-husband). The divorce was still not final (I had more important things to do). By this time I had been through one live-in boyfriend of three years, a shortcoming with another, and had dated others. I use dated lightly, they were more like booty-calls. Sure I have written about neglect, abuse, and abandonment through these pages but this path does end quite well. I say end as if there is also a new beginning. There are always new beginnings. We are creating new beginnings all the time. The path I write about now, in this book, is all about the Emerald Path, the path of the heart and learning to love. For me, this is the path to a true love, love of thine self. This Emerald Path has been about the breaking down of things I have put my soul through, the fucking lessons, and all of the pain. It is about the side roads I took and the adventures and risks I have taken. It is about all of this blood, these bruises, the laughter, the births, and the deaths. All of it has landed me right here, right now, with no regrets, but with an open heart full of forgiveness for myself and my actions.

I just keep on trucking with a grateful heart and positive thought. I have always known I would be okay, that I was loved by a higher power, and that I would always be led back in the right direction. My experiences go back to my early childhood, working my way to awakening. I accomplished this by writing, reading, and searching for truths and signs with a lot of faith. I did this by putting to use the gifts I was unwrapping, day by day, year by year. I connected with many things, just as you are connecting here with me now. You to seek to find your soul's destiny, your purpose.

I am so grateful you are now in this place, having the courage to pick up my book and read my story. Having the courage to connect to it in some weird way with. My wish for you is that you find some solace in your own journey by connecting with mine. Find the love within you and tell everyone to KISS YOUR PATH as well while Keeping Infinite Spirit Simple. It really isn't that far out of reach, you just have to keep your head clear, heart open, mouth wide, and see the world as it is; full of magic and mystery.

*Prior to perfection, one must experience and accept turmoil.*

*Fear is simply incomplete knowledge*

My experiences with The Great Divine, my vibrations, and my emotions have pushed me to my limits. With the help of my right-handed guardian, my inner Badger, and my loving aggressiveness, I too have begun to heal. The tools and gifts I have been offered through time have truly helped me to create who I am today. My weirdness inside is showing me how to speak and listen to my totem animals. The other gifts I also wish to share with you are the magic of Crystals and the vibrational energy, which they put off for us to use. When I do readings, I am up in the astral planes, with the Akashic records. My work with crystals has directed me to also learn about numerology and astrology. This was the next gift I unwrapped from God. These gifts would lead me to heal deeper and find the love of my life, my soul mate, and my co-creator in magic. Knowing what I know, connecting the

conscious mind via pen and paper, has directed me to my next

adventure with crystal healing, numerology, and astrology: the

healing vibrations to heal all levels of the mind, body, and spirit.

### THE MORNING SKY; FEBRUARY 13, 2017

The morning sky is beginning to rise

The purples, orange and blue hues.

Purple reminds of my spirituality, my fulfillment,
transforming me to my creativity and awareness.

Orange peeks through as the sun begins to rise.
Reminding me of my joy, my enthusiasm, and
creativity.

Gives me a great sense of wellness and confidence as
the sun rises to warm my body, to warm my soul.

Blue . . . to remind me to communicate my
inspirations, producing peace and calm as I awake
and send out my morning gratitude

The color blue which speaks to me for the next
awakening, next transformation as it soothes my
soul.

Much love and gratitude.. 333

Did you know that when we present our names in numbers, the numbers that are left out express our soul's experiences that are needed during this lifetime to assist the soul with manifesting our physical existence in this lifetime to complete this cycle? The numbers which are included in our names represent the minerals that support our accomplishments, the part of life that has happened. Each crystal or mineral vibrates to a specific number, and specific astrological sign(s). Each astrological sign and each planet have an associated numeric vibration as well. By learning these connections, we can open up a new type of healing to help us live our full soul potential and healthy lifestyles. These connections help us to complete and understand the experiences we need to help further our purpose. Excluded numbers can also help with health issues. I use a method in my holistic health practice that draws me to what information I need to access. This includes information for the seeker with direction on how to put the information to use. I use numerology (excluded numbers), astrology, and crystal/mineral information to channel what conditions in your current life may need attention or may need to be changed.

Crystals have been used for thousands of years throughout history. They work with our human energy fields. They move, absorb, and direct us to the energy needing healing, and they help us to find our body's natural rhythm. By the laying on of stones, the crystals and minerals give off vibrational healing onto the body in order to create change. Using numerology and excluded numbers points us to the right crystals and minerals needed for the individual healing. Doing so gives us access to the information the crystal or mineral holds and to what is needed in order to maintain good health.

Using astrology in the divine triage helps us to track health concerns as well as how to solve them. A term I AM beginning to use for my practice is Iatromathematics, which means the math of curing or medical mathematics. Being that I am a practitioner, I am not allowed to cure, so here I am only stating research terms. Our astrological sign gives us a look at our health as well. They can help us in determining the most beneficial foods and exercises on the individual level.

| 1 | 2 | 3 | 4 | 5 | 6 | 7 | 8 | 9 |
|---|---|---|---|---|---|---|---|---|
| A | B | C | D | E | F | G | H | I |
| J | K | L | M | N | O | P | Q | R |
| S | T | U | V | W | X | Y | Z | |

For example, Sue Smith is a name at birth. Excluded numbers in her name are 6 and 7. These are the experiences that Sue needs to facilitate for her soul to progress in this lifetime. Sue was also born under the astrological sun sign of Taurus. The mineral Amblygonite has a vibration of the number 6. This mineral is also under the astrological sign of Taurus. This tells me that Sue can use this stone to help her in pursuit of music, poetry, and the arts. She can use this to recognize the coexistence of opposite and conflicting feelings to resolutions of duality and ease any pain and enhance understanding when she is forced to end a relationship. It also gives me clues that Sue may be suffering from ambulatory disorders or vision concerns.

The minerals azurite, malachite, and chrysocolla can be combined to vibrate to 6 and astrological sign of Taurus. This mineral helps Sue to extend herself to others, in the spirit of love. It also provides assistance in promoting philanthropic tendencies.

There are many books out there to help you learn these techniques. My favorite is *Love is in the Earth. It is my crystal and mineral bible. I also use *Numerology and the Divine Triangle as a bible and tool. Both of these books have helped me to enhance my intuitive abilities and my holistic health practice.

Find what you like, use what you love. These tools and many others are available to us to tap into our own abilities. Find what you like, like what you love. It's all about accepting your gifts and using them for the most benevolent good to yourself and others if they come to you for assistance. Remember to do no harm and always ask for permission.

• Book citation in the back of the book

# Chapter Nine

# My Sunshine and Other Shiny Things

*This chapter is dedicated to my grandmother,*

*my sunshine.*

Like everyone else, I was born through the great vaginal descent. I landed right where I was supposed to. I was born to a single young mother of just sixteen years. I always joke and claim to be of Immaculate Conception from the virgin vessel. She claimed he pulled out. The "he" is my biological father, now in spirit. He passed before I was born before he even knew of my tiny existence. The vessel was just three months pregnant with me when he passed.

He was quite the rebel, so I have been told. His photos still remind me of Aidan Quinn. My youngest sister's youngest son is named Aidan Quinn. She didn't even know I had these thoughts about my father. It was just another synchronicity.

I often think my nephew is my father reincarnated; he has a limp in his foot as if he injured it. This was from an accident the poor little guy had with a nurse and a needle. We have so many other strange connections in my family. For example, there are shared birthdays, in threes. My youngest sister, my husband and my nephew share the same day. My other twin nephews and their dad share the same birthday, and another nephew shares his father's birthday. Then there is my daughter and my husband's nephew who both share a birthday. I love this stuff, numbers, and synchronism's are so much fun!

As it turns out, my father died in a plane accident while skydiving. He left us while traveling on a jet plane but he didn't know that he wouldn't return. The plane went down in Lake Henshaw, California, November 1964. All they found of him was his foot in a boot. I didn't learn about what happened until I was my thirties. Before this, I spent many years searching for any information I could find about what happened to him. The funny thing is that I grew up with the last name Marvin: my biological father's first name. I always had a weird feeling that the man who co-parented with the vessel for the first eleven years of my life never really did feel like my father. After all, we did not share any

DNA. His tribe always made me feel as though I was a part of the family, it is just that somehow I knew I wasn't a part of their DNA.

Grammy was my sunshine. She was my special safe place. She would always take me on trips down to southern California to see my Granny Goose, my great grandmother who lived with my great aunt and my second cousin David. He had MD but was always a ray of sunshine. We would sit and sing for hours and play the guitar. Probably not as well as I thought... the song we sang the most was "I am leaving on a jet plane . . . I don't know when I will be back again." See that? More synchronicity. "Oh baby, I hate to go." I understand the meaning of it all now, it was a song from my father.

Then there was my poor cousin. He suffered so much pain, but he was always happy and laughing. Even with his steady diet of Kaopectate. I can still imagine him with that stuff stuck in his teeth, gasping for air just to get out a joke. He was only supposed to live until the age of fourteen, but I'll be damned, he made it to Las Vegas on his twenty-first birthday, just like he said he would. Shortly after his twenty-first birthday, he did pass. I still think about him to this day. What sticks with me is that we don't leave this world until we have lived our wildest dreams. At least, that is how it was for him. Thank you, cousin, for sharing those tunes with me!

Another lesson I have learned in my life is that people get stupid when someone dies. My grandma died of a broken heart in 1993. Passed from being pushed to her limits. About a year had passed since my granddad passed from this life. My granddad had two older daughters from his first marriage; before marrying my grandmother. We used to tease and call Grammy a little hoochie mama. She was the housekeeper/babysitter in the household that was my grandfather's first marriage. His first wife had passed from dis-ease at a young age. He then married my grandmother. I used to tease her about being younger than my grandfather by about ten years.

After my granddad passed his older children yanked and pulled everything they could get their greedy hands on; furniture, vehicles, and family items that were to be passed down. I had an altercation with one aunt because they were ganging up on my grandmother. Trying to tell her what she had to give up. This aunt tried to put me in my place, but I was not having it; I stuck up for my grandmother. I got one of those finger shakes, "listen to me young lady." Ha! You don't get respect if you don't give respect. I lit into to her about her greed and all the stress she was putting on my grandmother. I told her to go to hell, even though I don't believe in hell, but if there were, she would go straight there.

My aunt's hurtful behavior ended up hurting her in some karmic way. I have a firm belief that disease is just that, a dis-ease, a term used in the holistic and wellness communities. I choose not to empower the other term. I choose not to give the other word power. My aunt ended up passing from a brain tumor, and so did her greedy daughter. All they could do was take, take, and take. They attempted to take my grandmother's home, a home she purchased. All for what? My great uncle used to always say; "You can't take it with you." I live by that. Greed is an intense and selfish desire for something. Well, that greed settled right on into my aunt's brain. Bless her soul.

My grandmother was so stressed by this that she ended up in the hospital. My sunshine had been taken away. Grandma was always hanging around though. She would leave me shiny things.

She used to love to use a metal detector, and us kids would throw pennies in the sand at the beach so she could find them; pennies from heaven, she knew what we were doing. It was pretty obvious, a bunch of little girls giggling, but she always acted surprised. After she passed, I would be walking along and would find pennies. Yep, it was she! That was her way of saying she was still with me. It eventually graduated to nickels, dimes, and then quarters. Make it rain, Grammy, make it rain!

The biggest shiny thing she brought to me was my husband. They actually all teamed up on me with this one. Gladys, my dad, and my grandma, that is, My Opinions. It was 1996, three years after she passed. I was so done with men. They were always using and abusing. Mostly for sex, control, and my soul. Those life sucking vampires. I was so tired and exhausted from men trying to control me, to take from me. I seemed to attract the creeps.

I did not want to go out this night, the fourth of July. He had been around me my whole life really. He lived in the Home Street neighborhood I grew up in. He lived in Modesto about the same time I lived there. He was an old friend's cousin's best friend

I had met just months before but had forgotten. At the time he was going through a separation as well. My best friend at the time talked me into going out to the neighborhood bar and play some pool. Well, we headed out: her, her boy toy, and myself. It ended up being one of the most magical nights of my life, right after the birth of my two bright and shiny stars, my kids.

We walked into a bar, (sounds cliché, I know): my BFF and her flavor of the day. We walked past the long bar, saying our hellos to the regulars as we passed. It was smoky and smelled of cheap beer with a shot of whiskey. The local hole in the wall. We walked into the pool table area, and I looked over to the left. About the third pool table in there stood a tall drink of water, good water. I saw this "good-looking thing, don't you ever die" type of guy.

I looked right at him and seemed as though time had stood still. There it is: there appears to be a bright and shiny halo surrounding his head. I shit you not, a halo. It was glowing and glorious. I looked over at my escorts and said, "I need to meet that man." The flavor of the day blurts out and says, "Oh so-n-so? I know him, I'll introduce you." Well, that was all it took. We haven't been separated since.

Now don't get me wrong, it hasn't been all rainbows and lollipops; but we ain't got to go nowhere, we have each other, we're connected. After crossing each other's paths for many years, we found one another, although I kid around and say, "I found you first." We had crossed each other's paths on many occasions before this. He stole the old man's "greenhouse" treasures back in the day on Home Street. We are still each other's heroes, and our relationship is still going strong. A trusted psychic once told us that a sorcerer and sorceress create great magic together, and we are still creating. My prince from "a place called home." He was living in the neighborhood back in the day.

I love shiny things, I have always been attracted to them. My husband calls me a crow. I have crow medicine, and you will see why in the next chapter.

*In loving memory and dedication to all my shiny*

*things. The Past, present, and my shiny future*

*Caw!!*

# Chapter Ten

# The Crow

*The crow is the left-handed guardian. The crow has a fascination with its shadow, the unknown, and mysteries. Crow can bend the laws in the physical world. It has rare and unique abilities and gifts. It is the keeper of sacred texts and universal law. This medicine holds the knowledge of a higher order.*

Being the "free" thinker that I am, I have not fit into most crowds during the span of my life. Most people I have come across thought of me as weird because of my gifts. My best subjects in grade school were English, easy math, and art. I like history, just not the history they taught in school. That is the made for TV kind of history.

I like the good stories, the true stories. I like stories of life, love, and death. You know, the truth. I am always seeking truths, hidden truths. My best years in school were the third grade and the ninth grade. I am a self-taught, natural born expert in everything. I prefer to learn my own way by digging into it, comparing, studying, and reading between the lines. Knowledge and wisdom are great tools and easy to practice. Don't ever just believe in something. Know and seek out things through inner knowledge and wisdom. Not the stuff you learn in school but your inner knowing.

Truths lie deep within our souls. We are vibration, energy, colors, and shiny things. Always look at things in a different way, change your view, and change your mind. One day you will look at something, and the next day it can change from what it was the first time you saw it. Our intentions one day may turn into something else the next. Once we begin to gain a new understanding of "I AM," creating becomes easier. One day you may intend to take out the trash, to unpack your baggage. The intention is the plan, the aim, and the purpose. Time goes by, and I AM taking out the trash, unpacking my baggage. I AM is NOW, not what I intend. Secrets and keys reside in words, and between words; one being a cause, the other an effect. Become the "U" in Universe. We are the god within. I am Christ within, I am the universe, and I am infinity. I am attracting to me what I need now.

I am attracting the vibrations I need to create. These are things we must say to ourselves. "I AM" is YOU doing, it is you NOW.

On Valentine's Day in 1997, we rented a house to move our little family into. It was the house on Wrenwood. The house on the crossroads. The kids called it the scary house because strange things happened there. We were able to rent this house by manipulating the physical world. We worked great magic together. I won't go into how we did that in order to protect our innocence. All sorts of weird things happened in this house. This particular day, Valentine's Day, was one the weirdest.

It was as if a stranger stepped into my body or I stepped out while I was napping. My husband noticed something strange: I was talking in my sleep. I could hear and see him arguing with this person. I felt as if I was stuck someplace, not in my body. I was in a white room with a window. Outside of this window were a green field and a single blue house. I opted to stay in the room. I could hear my husband arguing still, telling this person to leave. I was scared and wanted to leave this room, but not through the second story window. I could now see my husband as if we were separated by a glass-like wall. I began to bang on this wall, screaming at him to get me out. I was yelling at him, "I am here, I am right here, I am alive." Don't let me go I thought. It felt as if my husband was doing an exorcism, taunting this being. I felt so much sorrow and fear of not returning to my body. I felt as though I had died, or maybe a part of my being had. I was still pounding on the glass and having a hard time breathing. I was pounding even harder so he might hear me until finally the moment the glass seemed to have vaporized. I collapsed a bit. I was home, in my room.

Everything seemed to be in color again, bright colors. My husband was holding me, securing me. I was home. I could feel my heart warming and my breathing getting easier, but I was exhausted. It had seemed like forever. I had a slight pain in my hip and walked with a slight limp. We sat at the bottom of the staircase and hardly spoke of what happened. I was gaining some strength back. I walked into the kitchen to get some water. I looked over at our fish. The poor fish had somehow jumped out of its bowl and was lying on the kitchen counter, trying to catch its breath; it was still alive. I placed it gently back into its bowl. Was the fish trying to tell me something? I thought it wouldn't live as I had no idea how long it was out of the bowl, but it did.

I went back to the staircase and sat, waiting. The kids should be home from school soon. My son was the first one home. He was so excited to see mommy and to give me his Valentine card he made in class that day, he was just six. I began to read. It said on the front "HAPPY VALENTINE'S DAY." I opened it and read, "I love you." I took another look at it, and I could see faintly written under these words as if they had been erased. It said, "HAPPY VALENTINE'S DAY MOMMY, I love you, and I miss you." It was as if he wrote it as if I wasn't there. Fear came over me, and then joy stepped back in. I hugged him so tight for a long time. It was as if I had experienced two dimensions that day.

I don't know why or what happened that day. I do know I was not leaving this world. Not yet by the grace of God. Was this some kind of transition? Did my shadow wake up, and become alive? Was I being awakened and renewed so that I may know the unknowable mysteries? Crow is the sign of change and lives in the void.

This house became alive in many ways; weird ways, and not just on this day. The kids used to have many nightmares here. They would come running and knock on the bedroom door at night or jump into one another's beds. My eldest looked up at the empty neighbor house and could see a woman with a pearl necklace standing in the window. I saw her too. One time a friend and I went into the backyard of this house and looked into the windows. It was creepy. We looked at bricks on the outside of the fireplace and noticed that one was slightly pulled out. We opened it, and there was a credit card, a paper with numbers on it, and keys stuffed in there. We freaked out a little, shoved them back in, and ran back to the house. The next day we decided to go back to take another look, and the brick was sealed up.

My subconscious mind was really opening here in this house after the Valentine's Day event. There is a difference between "brain" and "mind." The brain is our three-pound organ in our head. The "mind" is something larger and more mystical. There is a big difference between our brains and minds. The subconscious mind is the source of thoughts supplied to the brain. While we are aware that we have a subconscious mind, there are very few of us who know much more than that about it. The trick is to harness it. This is unfortunate, for our subconscious mind can and should be a great ally in achieving success in your life. Trying to establish a working relationship with your subconscious mind can be a task. One must become conscious and familiar with what is hidden. See the magic. Use Crow medicine.

I do believe I may have opened up a bit too much in that house, but then again, once you begin to open, you can't go back. The things that came to me. For example, men were standing in my den. There were twelve of them, and they were wearing golden robes and holding staffs with candles. I would also read history books, and the characters would speak to me. I also began tapping into the Akashic records in that house. I did a lot of drawing and automatic writing, which was frightening at times to do. Not long after we moved from that house, I stopped. My mind needed a break, I needed some grounding. I needed to live in the moments and stop receiving. Something scared me into shutting down shop. I wasn't ready for this, not yet. I still had my gifts; I just closed the box for a while.

Everything I do now, I do for the love of my family: my husband and our kids. I have no regrets for the past, no sorrow. I have always had a forgiving nature. Not long after living on Wrenwood, we experienced adventures in homelessness and not being able to find work. We were living with friends at the time mostly because things were just not working out for us in that town. So we decided to move to Reno, for a fresh start. Fresno was getting bad. This was a difficult decision, and we faced some difficulty, of course.

There was the custody of children and getting them moved with us to Reno. I had to leave them to live with their father and grandparents in Fresno until their father and court had allowed me to move them out of the county. He could still be a huge ass, so we battled it out in court. He once accused me of kidnapping my children while they were on a visitation with me. I was taken to jail in front of my children just before a court hearing. I think that they all just felt sorry for him since he was "disabled." I did manage to get custody of my children. Through all the psychiatric evaluations and all, I would be whole again.

One day in Reno when the kids were in their teens, we had a knock on the door. It was the sheriff's department wanting to know if I had the kids because they were still reported as kidnapped. I called to the kids and said, "Guess what, you have been on a milk carton for the last few years." Of course they were with me! I had custody after all. I told them they could mark them as found.

*Life is easy, life is good*

*All good things come to me now*

*I deserve all good things that come to me and that*
*life has to offer*

*Now I know, now I AM*

I was feeling put back together after having moved to Reno and regaining custody of my children. I began writing again. While writing this book, I have been reflecting on my past journals to see just how much I trust in my gifts. I taught myself more about crystal vibrations and the Divine Triangle in numerology. I also

began using tarot a bit more. These are some of the divine tools I

use to get answers and the confirmations I need. I began to use all

these things together and found so much synchronicity in all of my

chosen modalities. One thing leads to another, a light goes off

directing me in such a way to move or search our the next clue.

I began taking courses in holistic health and herbalism.

Synchronizations are pre-programmed experiences that occur when

our DNA is programmed for a specific event in time. Something

happens and we react. We ponder or get all giddy inside. Then we

say "I must investigate further." You do, and then more

synchronizations occur, and you are suddenly following an

exciting line of action and reaction. This means that our souls are

sending us on a journey. Leaving us breadcrumb trails.

Crows have many meanings for me now, as you will read

further into the next chapter. I look back and consider where I am

now, I can see even more opening up and what those special

moments or events were there to teach me. We start to think we are

suffering from financial difficulties, yet money for basic expenses

always manifests. At first, you thank the universe or God, then you realize you created this abundance. We learn to watch how we manifest and why. You finally end a bad relationship and immediately another partner comes into your life as if by coincidence.

Or perhaps you feel depressed and can't focus. The next person you talk to says something that brings you some guidance in a whisper. In a world of wounded healers, and evolving consciousness, these answers help and guide us. We begin to learn to trust the sources that come to us. The magic word being "source." Access your soul by becoming coy with your inner guidance. Your soul is your guiding star. Practice meditation, write and listen to your inner voice. Crow may be coming to you from the void.

*Much love and gratitude*

*To all my totem spirit guides in the animal world*

*Thank you energy all around*

*Thank you void, thank you shadow, thank you light*

*Thank you snake, the Kundalini that rises inside*

*Snake medicine*

*Open me to God, to heal me once again*

*With the eternal flame and fire*

*Transmutation for my soul's desire*

# Chapter Eleven

## Sheet Music

Mr. Now and I currently live in Sonoma County. We decided to move after our youngest graduated high school. We have three children, separate, yet together. I am in an awakened state and still slowly awakening every day. This awakening is one reason that I am writing this book. It is a higher calling: the snake moves again. I called this chapter Sheet Music because it has to do with one of the ways God communicates with me: through the music, I wake up to in my dreams or just by driving in the car. One day I heard "You Are My Sunshine" all day, which led me to several things I needed to do, including this book.

Events are moving rapidly now as a result. I can't help but feel blessed for this gift. This is the gift that keeps on giving. Sheet music also comes from the sheets of my bed waking me in the morning or speaking to me during the day as the music plays. The music in our dreams always reminds us of each memory or each tragedy. These are the songs that run through my mind all day, sometimes even longer, like a broken record.

You are my sunshine is my reminder that I am blessed. It also reminds me of the bright, shiny sun. I am blessed to be able to sit here and write these words for you, telling my story, and sharing my gifts. Expressing how I use them as much as possible to create my life with a creative mind and a forgiving heart. It reminds me to get to work and write down the thoughts that are being given to me daily, to get them onto paper. It reminds me to capture all of the latest signs and omens that happen around me for the day. All the ideas, inventions, and words that sprout up in our minds; get them down onto the sheets of paper. Create your own music. All thoughts, that if put into action, can create success in our lives. Positive thoughts that run through your mind and loving vibes do no harm. Write down the ideas you want to use to get to your own joy and abundance.

My current career choice is in the tech industry. I was an implementation specialist for Point of Sale software. If I were having a hard time figuring out a programming issue I had been troubleshooting, I would walk away for a while (usually the whole day). Most likely that night the answer would come to me in my dreams and the next day my issue was solved! My motto is "I can fix it because I know how it works." Sheet music usually works the same way for me. I usually go to bed and wake up with an idea or song to my waking day. This doesn't happen every night, it's not always the sound of music up there, and I have had my share of nightmares too. I visit my ancestors and past lives in my dreams, I feel pain in my dreams. They are so real that I sometimes wake up in pain. But I am quite fond of the sheet music anyway.

One morning in 2016, the song "Hello" by Adele played in my head over and over and over. This was very special music to my ears. You see, I was just about to leave for a weekend trip to Southern California. An exciting trip had been planned. My love, my soul mate, gave me a great surprise for Christmas in 2015. He purchased tickets to fly down to Southern California. The year 2015 was so full of newfound family connections. I had gifted my family with a reading for my birthday this same year. A lot of folks came through; it was a joyous day. My father came through. He said that he was sorry he left so soon, and he loves me. Words I was longing to hear and had not heard before. I knew who was coming to this event in spirit. Similarly, a week before this our youngest and I had received a mysterious phone call. The person had asked about our departed Jerry. Jerry was my brother-in-law who had just passed. The weird thing was that nobody had our phone numbers, especially our daughter's phone number. She had a brand new phone number. He also showed up in the reading we did that day. Then there was the water jug. The lid would vibrate and want to pop off, someone wanted to let us know they were all showing up to the party.

Hello, Spirit was calling. I had connected with a lot of cousins on my father's side in 2015 and two of my father's sisters that are still living. The flight took us down to meet my cousins and one of my aunts. This trip was truly a blessing. My husband arranged the trip for us to go down to meet them all. He made arrangements for a family gathering and dinner. What a reunion this was.

I woke up to that song every day for a week before and during the visit. This was one of the best gifts I could have asked for. Mr. Now actually surprised me for once. I had no idea about this year's gift (I could usually guess). I had been searching for family for years on my father's side, and here I was with seventeen of them at the dinner table. My aunt, my father's baby sister, having been in a convalescent home at the time, met with me for the first time. I remember her piercing blue eyes. It was as if she had been waiting to hear from me for years. She knew I existed, but sometimes I think, why did no one ever attempt to reach out and find me? I may never have that answer, I'm not really sure I even care.

When the vessel was three months pregnant with me, in 1964, she called my aunt. I later found out that they both share the same birthday. My aunt told me she remembered that phone call. The vessel was just sixteen at the time. My aunt had bad news for her. She was given the message that my father had passed, died in a horrific plane crash; and that only a foot was found and identified. I can only imagine how she might have felt. Alone is the first word that comes to mind. The thing I don't get is why they never communicated after that; maybe those answers will come soon. However it may be, I am okay with it. We do our best with the hand we have dealt ourselves, with the helping hands of God.

We drove to the convalescent home to meet my aunt. It was as if she had been waiting to meet me her whole life. We spoke as much as we could. She was quite debilitated. She asked if I had any questions. I did not have many at that time, none that had not already been answered. It just felt good to be in the presence of someone who had been in the presence of the immaculate one, The Mighty Quinn, the rebel without a cause. You get the picture. All these words perfectly describe the photos of I have of him: photos in his flight suits, by old cars, smoking a cigarette. We were looking at photos as she explained whom each of her brothers and sisters was.

One Aunt, in particular, popped out at me, her name was Gladys. My cousin has told me I reminded him of her. I had Granny Goosebumps. I was given such a great gift that day. That evening we had dinner planned with the cousins, some of her children, some his brother's children, and grandchildren. What a dinner this was, the whole famdamily. We took up a whole banquet room in the upstairs of an Italian Restaurant. There was a lot of laughter and a few tears. I told myself I wasn't going to cry. Well, I sobbed! One of my cousins, under strict demands from my aunt, brought me a gift. It was one of my dad's old and cherished toys. It was a "made in Japan" Santa about three inches high. It was a nice reminder of the child he was because I still believe in Santa. It still has a place in my living room, under a glass dome, which is a timeless reminder.

They also shipped his old radio to me, with the old tubes and all. It is stuck on the song Hello; at least in my head whenever I look at it. One thing that also sticks with me is something my cousins told me. They spoke of our grandpa Frank and how hard he took it when my father died. He would sit outside, roll a cigarette, and have a beer. He would see a single crow in the yard, and he would say that crow was Marvin, my dad. I think he was right. I have a murder of crows in my yard. I adore them. They are my family and a constant reminder.

That Monday after arriving home on Sunday, You are my Sunshine played in my head again. Thank you, Grammy! Thank you for waking me up on that glorious morning to tell yet another part of my story. This is a good memory and a blessing. It is a reminder of one of my many gifts: my sheet music. It is a reminder that we have guides with us at all times. Take your gifts and use them to reach your atonement, purpose, and abundant prosperity as I have. Life has many gifts. It's all about how you unwrap them. You just have to start picking at the tape and then reach inside. You may have more than one. At least show up to receive them. Don't leave the partygoers waiting, you are the guest of honor. We all arrive at our purpose, whatever that may be.

# Chapter Twelve

## Let Go of My Ego

The year was 2001, and we were living in Reno. I had a great job and a great life overall. It was a time of letting go, of transcending the ego. Even through all my past tragedies, I still had a bit of an ego. The ego really isn't a bad thing or something to fear. I believe it can just be misguided at times. I was building myself back up again, feeling human, successful, and alive. I feel there was a part of me that got jealous, self-conscious, anxious, and fearful. The ego wishes to protect us from life's doings, and I had not fully let go of the past yet. It was unhealthy and at times a bit painful to hold onto that. I was not truly authentic to myself or to my gifts.

I was a boss at a casino in the food and beverage department, and a damn good one. But this wasn't me; it is what I did to make a living and a life for my family. Then there were all those bright casino lights. My psychic friend once told me to stay away from these bright lights, and I went flying right into them.

She said these lights throw off your auras and clog your energy. I truly believe they do. It was exhausting working there at times.

We are love. We are here to be loved. Sometimes we allow our egos to define this love instead of letting our souls do it. We don't need to be loved or need love, we are love. That is, I AM love. The needing is a concept given to us through ego. We seek approval, and that approval allows us to seek out those vampire types as significant others, booty calls and so-called friends. Often times this turns into us becoming victims. I AM a survivor, not a victim. I was attracted to my soul mate, and still am for that matter, because he always allows me to be me and encourages my inner wild woman. No control, no approval necessary. I guess that is why opposites attract. We balance each other out in so many ways even though people said it wouldn't last. I state that without ego, I state that because I am proud, and I state it out of love.

Let us get back to the year 2001. When I had what I call 'the chip on my shoulder". Yeah, that's right, go ahead, knock it off. I dare you. Words have power, so we must all be careful what we wish for. I was holding on. Mr. Now noticed it but I hadn't. Mr. Now forced me to have it looked at by our family physician.

I made my appointment with the family doctor. The appointment was to look at a sizable black mole on my right shoulder. I thought nothing of it since I have moles all over my body. I never thought to look at them. My doctor decided we needed to get a biopsy. I was lucky that I visited my doctor on that day because his in-house dermatologist just happened to be there. He called for her to come in and take a look. She did. I was getting a biopsy that day, in the office. They prepped me with local anesthesia. She cut into me pretty good; good enough, that I had more than a dozen stitches.

Now that part of this chip was gone, my mind was combative with all sorts of thoughts. Had I been holding a grudge? You betcha! Was I holding on to some anger? Oh yeah. This piece went out for biopsy, that was the longest week or more I have ever had to wait for news. Finally, the doctor's office called while I was at work. They had some news for me. They asked me all kinds of questions to verify that they had the right person. It was melanoma.

Time stood still. I began to silently cry. It was a long conversation with explanations, but all I could remember was garbling sounds and melanoma. Finally coming to my senses, but still sobbing, I made my next appointment to remove the chip. I call it the chip because I do not like to place the M word or C word to it. I believe that it was a dis-ease and not a disease. I choose not to empower the D word. I like to empower the thought that I simply had a lack of ease or harmony within my body and the chip was a transmutation of that.

So the appointment finally came, the day of removal. Take it away please, I have no use for it any longer. So they did. Local anesthesia? Check. Cutting tools? Check. After an hour or so of careful removal and two sets of stitches--I believe there were thirty-four inside and out-- digging deep into my shoulder, it was out. It was in a jar, I said my goodbyes. Now the fun part: it needed to be checked to be certain the whole thing was out, roots and all. So I had to wait some more. My doctor had also ordered me to see a specialist and have some blood work and scan testing completed for good measure.

I made my appointments and went back to my doctor to get the news. It turned out that they did manage to cut it all out. However, I had my scan and blood work yet to do. I jump in the machine, then I jump out, and head home. I get home, and the lab called me and said I needed to come back. They spotted something on my rib cage. Fear rushed through my body, but I kept telling myself it would be okay. So my husband and I drove back to the lab. While sitting in the waiting room once again, I couldn't help but begin to sob. This was scaring me. They called my name, and I went back into the scanner. I jumped back in, jumped back out, and waited for the results. I was trying hard not to cry anymore. They came out to give me the results, and it turns out to be a bit of calcium build up from what looked to be a crack in ribs. What a relief! And then the memory came flooding back from that day.

The day I lay on the floor of my home being repeatedly kicked. All that doesn't matter now. I am alive, and I am love. Little Chippers is gone, gone for good.

I have been free of Chip for over seventeen years now. My scars are deep, but I am love. I let go of my ego. Whenever you find yourself in conflict, notice what you are feeling while also remembering who you really are. Notice if you are acting out of a need for approval or control. Take notice of judgments then take a look in the mirror. Take a step back and view how your ego may

be misguiding you. Take a deep breath, then let go of your ego.

# Chapter Thirteen

# The Heart Wants

Your heart wants what it wants. Your Heart's Desire is the inner you. It shows your underlying urges, your true motivation. It reveals the general intentions behind many of your actions. It dramatically influences the choices you make in life. The Heart's Desire is a big part of the larger picture. Ask yourself what emotional memories still need to be healed? What relationship needs to be healed? What fears are holding you back? Who or what needs to be forgiven to release the pain we hold onto? The day you were born is very closely connected to learning about your life's path and the healing lessons that you have asked to walk with. It reveals specific talents you possess, which are helpful to you in dealing with your Life Path. The Heart's Desire manifests into the identity of the soul that joined you here on earth - you, the spiritual being.

Deep inside you long to create something that will have a lasting impact on the world. Whether it is a political movement, business, craft, or philosophy, you have a strong inner drive to manifest something of major importance. The heart's desire is all that possesses the intelligence, sensitivity, and electric creativity that such a power would suggest. This combination can make you supremely capable of making your ambitions a reality. The demands of this Heart's Desire are as enormous as its potential. What will be required from you to fulfill your noble ambitions is nothing less than a commitment to your entire being. The path you have chosen is not an easy one. We all need time to develop, and you are likely to begin to fulfill your ambitions once your heart's desire has been met.

Whether you know it or not, you possess great power. You were born with this inherent power, and on some level, you are always aware of it. If you picked up this book, some part of you is aware. Early in my life, this power manifested itself in me as awkwardness and internal discomfort. My self-image has always been one of the contradictory extremes: on the one hand, I sensed my uniqueness and potential; on the other, I felt insecure and perhaps even inferior. This paradox has caused me waves of self-doubt and lack of confidence. But it has also created a powerful generator of energy in me that when combined with God, can become a dynamic and unrelenting force. In order to channel such great power, we need a noble goal to aim for. You will probably try your hand at several different kinds of work before you rise to the challenge of your true ambitions. But promise yourself you will try.

We can become great leaders and teachers inspiring and motivating others with our vision with an open heart and open mind. Our ideas are so creative and paramount that they inspire enthusiasm. Once we come into possession of our full power of creativity, without becoming arrogant, we can become the best at what we do and what path we take to create our Heart's desires. Your challenge, once you have begun to use our true gifts, is to remain humble in the face of your accomplishments. We perform best when our domestic foundations are stable and supportive, and we are able to share our dreams with those we trust and love. Let loving challenges draw out the best in you. Our human qualities - creativity, humility, understanding, and compassion can and will increase our level of our performance. Therefore, commitment to excellence is central to our success and inner development in creating our heart's desires.

Your Heart Center, your heart chakra, the chakra of balance is a good place to begin. It is located between the earth and the spiritual chakras. It is the home of unconditional love, and when it becomes unbalanced, we are unable to forgive and release resentments, grief, anger, hope, and trust. Its color is a luscious green embodying the love of mother earth with an airy and light energy movement. If you meditate, the mantra for chanting is the YAM seed sound, (you are my sunshine). The words from your lips sealed with a kiss are I LOVE or I AM LOVE. If done correctly, you can sense it opening up our ability to give and receive.

Love is divine power. Namaste!

# Chapter Fourteen

## Awaken The Snake

Kundalini energy led me to write this book. It is a process of transmutation of all that life pitches at us, which is why I started at the heart. This was part of what needed to be healed first. Six is the number of the snake, the Kundalini, the life force. It is an acceptance of past actions, the eternal flame, and compassion that opens us up to God to heal us. WE are universal beings.

I believe a lot of the mental illness in the world has to do with blocked Kundalini and the inability to handle the transformations happening between Kundalini movements. Every human on this planet is creative. Some are able to harness their creativity more than others. Others tend to fight it not knowing what it is and the energy it can put out. Some can become a danger to themselves and others through this denial.

I believe we need to teach more people how to self-soothe rather than medicate. I have always thought that if I told anyone I could work with energy, I would be deemed crazy, even though crazy was my middle name. But I could, I could stop a gate from opening; I could make the frogs stop singing only to begin their orchestra of their croaking again. People have witnessed this. I could will a person to fall out of his chair and hit his head whenever I was angry. I haven't done any of this in a long time for the sake of being called out on it, just for the sake of questioning my ability. It doesn't work that way. Actually, I don't really know how it works, it just works. It works when I most want it to, and it is not to be used for showing off. But hey, who am I but a little weird. I always have been. In alchemy, the goal is to transmute base metal into gold. I used to make jewelry. I wrapped crystal jewelry. At one point I needed to sell a piece badly to buy food, so I concentrated wholly on this piece and made it glow gold. It brought in enough money to put food on the table for a week.

I now practice other magical gifts: the gift of creating bigger things in life, and it's about time. After all of the rising of my inner serpent, it is finally coming into perspective. Transformation is a bitch! At least it has been for me. I sometimes thought I would end up in a loony bin. For the sake of God and my children, I would not allow it. I AM sane, creative maybe, but always sane. I will not forsake my gifts any longer. I choose to share them now in hopes of assisting in the awakening of the tribe: the rainbow tribe here on the green earth. The Emerald City in the circle of life. The tribe is waiting and awakening one by one, tribe by tribe for the sake of Ascension. Ascension to the next level or dimension is the ascension to our home, a new home in the infinity of homes. Hopefully, I will leave a legacy pointing to this home, because you always go back home once you know the way. This is the way of the travelers following maps, using their tools, gifts, and adventures.

It's time for fellow travelers to awaken and tell the tales of their own travels. It is time again to decipher truths. It is time to read between the lines, it is all there, already mapped for us. Get out of your bubbles and look around. There are gifts all around like hunting eggs on Ostera. I have enough stories to keep me going until I am very old. I am and will create from now on. I will myself to tell stories and to advocate for others to tell their stories. Create safe spaces for those of the same mind seeking their own truths for the right hand of God, and the creative left minds are mightier than the sword. Only cowards choose war, like little children throwing fits. We are the creative forces to shine through the illusion. This is the universal law of cause and effect. To put it another way, you can bullshit the tourists, but you can't bullshit the natives. Put actions behind your words, the definition of what it is to create.

I am still learning how God so created the earth and let there be light. I will begin those conversations and converse more, so stay tuned. It is all a mystery.

*Dear God,*
*What's next? I will be listening. I AM creating.*

# THANK YOU GOD!

# THANK YOU ALL

To my kids: all three of you. I love you, and yes, Mom is bat-shit crazy, that won't change and neither will the chicken music. XO.

To "Mr. Now": For always reminding me that LOVE is truly all you have. For seeing the "chip" on my shoulder, and being there for me when it was removed. Thank you for being my One Headlight through the fog and for showing me what wicked is. Thank you for not judging me, for being my drinking buddy and best friend. I love you. The fantasies are gone, but the dream lives on because we make great magic together.

To my sisters: for always looking up to me and asking for advice. It wasn't what you always wanted to hear, but one thing I am is honest. I love you and the women you have become.

To MOM: (the vessel), thank you for being the vessel that brought me into this world through your Immaculate Conception. Thank you for the tools you have gifted me to help me find my path, I am always grateful. Thank you for letting me call you on the carpet in my book. You are and always have been a gentle soul. You are a little bag of mixed nuts, but nonetheless gentle. Much love and gratitude.

To Jacob Nordby: thank you. For without the book Blessed Are the Weird I would not have opened up to my weirdness yet again.

To my editor: Sean Avila Saiter Ph.D., thank you for setting my words straight and giving me a bit more divine play and Poetic License.

http://drsaiter.com/psychological-consulting

# ABOUT THE AUTHOR

CJ has a passion for the healing arts and possesses a creative weirdness since she was a child. She adores anything magical, healing, sounding and colorful. With study and practice in anything and everything holistic, intentional, magical and weird.

CJ has certifications in Holistic Health, Holistic Nutrition, and is a Master Herbalist. She is has a B.Msc and is an ordained Minister. She is always working to further her spiritual journey. CJ has many interests including divinity, numerology, astrology, sound therapy, genealogy, and true history.

Christine's creative force is wanting to connect with those of you seeking the same vibrational energy in search of our soul's destiny. She has found hers and will continue to be amazed by it and its ever-changing amazement.

By sharing her story, she can only hope to have awakened something in you.

A statement from Christine Janette:

This book was written by me, lover of nature, a nonconformist, speaking and writing with my native tongue and thoughts. I put it through one professional edit to retain my Poetic License. This is a real-life story that has encountered struggles, and kisses from spirit, from God.

I created this life so that I am able to share it with you through creative writing. We create our realities so that we can share our creations in order to release fears and limitations. Create a life of unconditional love and plenty of kisses from God.

If you view any mistakes in this book, please email me at cjbadger333@gmail.com

# Citations

**book citations

Love is in the Earth, by Melody: Earth Love Publishing

Numerology and the Divine Triangle, by Faith Javane and Dusty Bunker: Whitford Press

www.ingramcontent.com/pod-product-compliance
Lightning Source LLC
Chambersburg PA
CBHW071054040426
42443CB00013B/3334